Using Children's Literature to Learn About Disabilities and Illness

Joan K. Blaska
Professor of Child and Family Studies
St. Cloud State University

Practical Press
PO Box 455
Moorhead, MN 56561-0455
(218) 233-2842

Library of Congress Cataloging in Publications Data

ISBN: 1-886979-07-3

Table of Contents

About the Author

Dr. Blaska is a Professor in the Department of Child and Family Studies at St. Cloud State University in St. Cloud, Minnesota. Dr. Blaska teaches family courses and early childhood methods for children with and without disabilities. She also coordinates the early childhood special education licensure program. *Using Children's Literature to Learn About Disabilities and Illness* is the result of four years of research in the area of children's literature that includes a character with a disability or illness. Dr. Blaska frequently presents at state and national conferences and consults extensively with early childhood programs on curriculum issues and working effectively with families who have children with disabilities.

Dedication

Special thanks to my colleague, Dr. Evelyn Lynch, Associate Dean at Teacher's College, Ball State University, Muncie, Indiana who was Co-investigator on our first grant funded project that looked at popular children's literature for the inclusion and depiction of individuals with disabilities. An additional thanks to the parents and professionals who were critical reviewers of those children's books. That initial project developed the *Images and Encounters Profile* that this author used in further research which identified and reviewed a variety of children's books that had a character with a disability or illness and culminated in this publication.

Introduction

This book is designed to help parents and early childhood professionals teach young children about disabilities through children's literature. It is specifically designed for teachers in Nursery Schools, Montessori, Head Start, Early Childhood Family Education, Early Childhood Special Education, Early Intervention, Kindergarten, Primary Grades, Parent Education, as well as Child Care Providers, Librarians, Child-life Specialists and Support Staff who work with children this age (i.e. Occupational Therapists, Physical Therapists, Speech/Language Clinicians).

All children should have the opportunity to learn about diversity of ability much like they learn about cultural diversity. Yet, often this does not happen. When surveying parents and professionals about their knowledge and use of disability literature for young children, the findings indicated that they did not know what literature was available. In addition, Blaska and Lynch found that many professionals tended to include literature about a disability only when a child with that disability became a member of their class. Children should be learning about disabilities and illness throughout the curriculum and throughout time so that when they have the opportunity to interact or be classmates with someone with a disability they have some previous knowledge and understanding. Many of the professionals who participated in the surveys indicated that they would be interested in using more books in their programs if they knew which ones were available and appropriate to use. This book was written to make the task of finding literature about disabilities and illness easier for parents and professionals (Blaska & Lynch, 1991).

Over 175 books were reviewed and rated. Based on the review of each book using the *Images and Encounters Profile,* each book was rated as outstanding, very good, fair or not recommended. One hundred forty of these books were then selected to be included in this collection. An annotated bibliography was developed for each book to make it easier for you to choose books that include the type of information or characters that you want. Cross-referencing was done to facilitate the ease in which a title can be located.

The books include fiction and nonfiction, represent ten disability areas and six chronic illnesses. All books are for the early childhood population. Early childhood includes children from birth to age eight based on the definition of the National Association for the Education of Young Children (NAEYC).

The majority of books have been published since 1985 with 66 books published since 1990. Most of the books are available at book stores and libraries, however, in the event you are unable to locate a specific title, a list of publishers is provided in Appendix B. Anyone working with young children will find this book to be a valuable resource.

The first chapter emphasizes all of the learning that takes place through the use of literature including learning about people with disabilities or illness. It stresses the importance of using literature that incorporates diversity of ability as well as of culture; especially with inclusionary programs and the emphasis on whole language and literacy approaches.

Chapter Two is intended to increase the reader's understanding of how to read aloud to young children. Hints for reading aloud effectively are included. Chapter Three is designed to help the reader teach about common differences which generally precedes teaching about disabilities. Included is a short annotated bibliography of books about differences that would be fun to use when teaching the concepts of same and different.

Chapter Four provides information on how to teach about disabilities and chronic illness to young children. Strategies for teaching are outlined with information on how to spiral it throughout the curriculum. The philosophy of using "person first" language when talking about people with disabilities is presented. The belief is that in order to demonstrate respect, it's important to talk about individuals with disabilities first as people and then to address the disability if in fact discussion of it is a necessary part of the conversation. Many examples are provided encouraging the reader to adopt this philosophy. Demonstrating respect and dignity as you teach children is also stressed. In order to answer children's questions about a disability or illness it's necessary to have some basic information. A brief overview is provided for 16 disabilities and six chronic illnesses. How to respond to young children's questions is a part of each overview.

Chapter Five outlines the process that was used to select the books for this project as well as describing the review and rating system. The development of Book Categories and the Theme Analysis that was conducted on each book are also discussed. Chapter Six reviews all of the components of the annotated bibliographies. This is followed by the "Annotated Bibliography of Books Depicting Persons With Disabilities or Chronic Illness." The annotations will give you a brief overview of the story plus additional information that will help you in making an appropriate selection for your child or students.

Chapter Seven contains a Book List of the children's books cross-referenced by disability and chronic illness. When you need a book about a specific disability or illness this bibliography will make the job an easy one. Chapter Eight has the books cross-referenced according to how the disability or illness is treated within the story. The books are divided into three categories according to this treatment and will give you additional information in making your book selection.

Chapter Nine describes the Theme Approach which is used by most early childhood professionals. This is followed by the books cross-referenced by

Theme. When teaching with a specific theme, merely turn to this bibliography to find which books can be used that incorporate disability or illness.

The final Chapter 10 provides Lesson Plans for 48 Themes to help the reader organize the children's literature that he or she chooses to use with each Theme. The disability literature that is appropriate for each Theme has been entered in a format that allows the reader to continually update the lesson plan with newly found books.

An appendix with activities for teaching about disabilities, publishers of children's books, the children's books listed by title, and disability organizations and resources is provided at the end of the text.

Notes

CHAPTER ONE

Why It's Important to Teach All Children About Disabilities and Chronic Illness

Introduction

Books serve as mirrors for children to see characters who look and have feelings and experiences similar to their own. Books also serve as windows through which children learn about their world by looking beyond their immediate surroundings and seeing characters and events that occur in other parts of the world (Rudman & Pearce, 1988). It is through books that children are able to learn about and make sense of what goes on in their world (Sawyer & Comer, 1991). The images of people and places that children form from their earliest literacy experiences are recognized as important for their overall development. In children's books, young children need characters with whom they can identify (Rudman & Pearce, 1988). Within the stories, they need to see familiar experiences and emotions (Hall, 1987).

In literature, children need to encounter a variety of role models that represent the diversity of people in the society and world in which they will grow up (Routman, 1988). Children with disabilities or illness need to see people similar to themselves. Perhaps no group has been as overlooked and inaccurately presented in children's books as individuals with disabilities. Most often they were not included in stories and when they were many negative stereotypes prevailed such as characters who were pitiful or pathetic, evil or superheroes, or a burden and incapable of fully participating in the events of everyday life. Often the difference or disability was the main personality trait emphasized to the reader; not a balance of strengths and weaknesses (Blaska & Lynch, 1994).

Over the past fifteen years, authors, illustrators and publishers have made an effort to develop more positive role models (Rudman & Pearce, 1988). Included in these efforts have been the inclusion of characters from a variety of socioeconomic levels, life-styles and heritage (Routman, 1988). However, it should be remembered that diversity is not limited only to heritage. Characters with disabilities need to be included to represent the population with varying abilities.

A study by Blaska and Lynch in 1992 reviewed 500 award-winning and highly recommended books for children, birth to age eight and published between 1987 and 1991, for the inclusion and depiction of persons with disabilities. Of the books that were reviewed, ten (2%) included persons with disabilities in the storyline or illustrations. Within the ten books, persons with disabilities were integral to the storyline in only six of the books. The limited presence of persons with disabilities was surprising and points out the need for more stories that represent the diversity of society which includes persons with varying abilities.

Influence of Books and Reading

According to the latest research findings, attitudes can be changed by reading or being read stories (Sawyer & Comer, 1991). Schrank and Engles (1981) reviewed the literature on bibliotherapy which is sometimes called guided reading and found that the research overwhelmingly supports the premise that guided reading can bring about attitudinal changes toward disabilities.

Bibliotherapy simple means using books and subsequent discussions to address a variety of needs. This process can be used at all ages and can be effective with very young children. There can be many benefits such as clarifying misconceptions, understanding yourself and other people, and developing self-confidence. Care should be taken in the appropriate selection of books and in the presentation of the content (Sawyer & Comer, 1991). A study by Salend and Moe (1983) challenged the notion that exposure to children's books about disabilities alone can affect a positive attitude change. However, when books were paired with activities that highlight the critical information to be learned, books became highly successful in changing attitudes. The results of this study point out the importance of children participating in discussion or activities following the reading of stories.

Literature about disabling conditions can help children understand and accept persons with varying abilities. The Carnegie Corporation (1974) findings are still relevant today, "Books, perhaps children's books most of all, are powerful tools by which a civilization perpetuates its values - both its proudest achievements and its most crippling prejudices. In books children find characters with WHOM they identify and whose aspirations and actions they might one day try to emulate; they discover, too, a way of perceiving those who are of a different color, who speak a different language or live a different life" (p. 1).

Brothers and Sisters

When one of the children in a family has a disability or illness, it has an effect on all members of that family including the brothers and sisters. The siblings often do not understand what is happening. Brothers and sisters generally have a number of questions, concerns, and fears. Many stories about families who have children with disabilities or illness exist that can help parents tell their story. There are a number of books that address the issues of living with a child with a disability or illness. In these stories, siblings are able to see that they are not alone with the questions and feelings they have. Through these stories they can learn about themselves as well as their brother or sister. Reading stories such as these opens the door for healthy discussion where siblings can get their questions answered, heighten their understanding of the child with the disability and help them feel better about themselves.

Reading literature can help children understand their feelings and develop a sense of self. When children read about others who are trying to make sense of a situation similar to their own, it brings hope. Children learn that their feelings are typical, which helps them understand that they are okay people even if they have those feelings. It helps them understand that there is no need for guilt which can lower their sense of self esteem. Through empathetic characters in literature, children can learn tolerance for others. They can learn through characters in the stories how to develop solutions to problems. (Sawyer & Comer, 1991). Books can be inexpensive yet powerful tools for providing information to siblings.

Inclusionary Programs

Best practices currently dictate that young children with disabilities should be educated with their peers who do not have disabilities (Sainato & Lyon, 1989). Several laws have provided the impetus to educate children with disabilities in the regular classroom. Educating children in integrated settings better prepares them for living in a heterogeneous society. Positive attitudes about human differences can be promoted through inclusionary programming. This increases the possibility for positively influencing societal attitudes towards people with disabilities (Safford, 1989).

The children of today are the future parents of children with disabilities or illness. They will become the future classmates, neighbors, doctors, teachers, coaches, families and so forth. Children who learn about people with differences at an early age and learn to accept those differences will become citizens who are more sensitive, tolerant and understanding of people of all abilities. Children tend to be afraid of the unfamiliar. Once children have the opportunity to interact and be educated with children with disabilities they will be exposed to a variety of differences and common fears can be overcome.

There is a tendency for professionals to use books about a particular disability or illness when they have a child with that particular need in their program. While this has merit, books from the disability literature should be incorporated into every program and not be limited to classes where a child with a disability is a member. This is the only way to educate all children about a variety of abilities and disabilities. With exposure through literature, children will have some knowledge and preparation prior to meeting a person with a disability or illness whether it's in school or in the community.

Literacy and Curricular Emphasis

In many of the integrated programs, early literacy practices include the whole language approach. This is a literature-based approach to teaching language that immerses students as much as possible into real life situations and the variety of communication that is utilized. This approach supports the concept of emergent literacy which focuses on the natural growth and development of both reading and writing. In this approach, oral and written language are kept whole, not fragmented into parts. Children learn that words have meaning in their environment. They learn important words in their environment that have meaning to them instead of focusing on learning names of letters or sounds in isolation. (Froese, 1991).

The whole language approach means that the four main areas in language arts, listening, speaking, reading and writing, are taught together in an integrated manner. In this approach, through a variety of activities which includes the reading of books, children are able to see how spoken language is related to reading and writing and vice versa. For example, children might listen to a story such as *The Three Little Pigs*. Later, the children might act out the story or use puppets to tell the story. This shows the relationship between reading and speaking (Stephens, 1994). It's important that all of the children are introduced to a diversity of characters as books are used in the classroom. This should include persons with disabilities. Children who have disabilities or illnesses need to be able to see people like themselves in some of the stories that are read.

Bias Free Curriculum. Schools are making every effort to have bias free schools that use an antibias curriculum. An antibias curriculum reflects diversity of race and ability and non stereotypic gender activities. This bias free philosophy should be reflected in the materials used by having a balance among different groups of people, and a balance of men and women doing a variety of jobs that do not stereotype by sex. People with varying abilities should be depicted as doing work and participating in recreational activities with their families being careful not to create images of dependency and passivity (Derman-Sparks, 1991).

Today, publishers of children's books do not accept manuscripts with obvious bias toward race, religion, ability, sex, or age. However, there are many books published in past years that do contain negative bias and some books with subtle bias. When using books with young children it's important that they be previewed for forms of bias which may influence how the books are used.

Often collections of books have bias by omission. To determine if this is happening, simply count the number of books, determine how many of the books represent the various kinds of people and look at the number that represents the people that you are checking. You will be able to see if there is a representative number of books. There is no magic number, but the ratio should tell you if there is a need for concern (Sawyer & Comer, 1991). It's important that all children see themselves in materials that are being used in the classroom. This means that children with disabilities or illnesses need to see books that have characters like themselves.

Whole language and literacy approaches are dominant teaching strategies for young children with and without disabilities in integrated programs. If parents and professionals are to foster positive relationships between children and enhance the self-esteem of children with disabilities, it's important that role models and activities in which the children participate be inclusive, realistic and positive ones (Blaska & Lynch, 1991). Society is changing and is becoming more accepting of people who are different. We can promote this acceptance by carefully planning how we work with young children.

References

Blaska, J.K., & Lynch, E.C. (1994). *Inclusion and depiction of individuals with disabilities in award-winning and highly recommended children's books.* Manuscript submitted for publication.

Blaska, J.K., & Lynch, E.C. (1991). *Images and encounters: Inclusion and depiction of individuals with disabilities in award-winning books, recommended books and children's classics.* Unpublished manuscript.

Blaska, J.K., & Lynch, E.C. (1991). *Let's Think About Books.* Unpublished manuscript.

Carnegie Corporation. (1974). Racism and sexism and children's books. *Carnegie Quarterly,* 22 (4), 1-8.

Derman-Sparks, L. (1991). *Anti-bias curriculum: Tools for empowering young children.* Washington, DC: NAEYC.

Froese, V. (1991). *Whole-language: Practice and theory.* Boston, MA: Allyn and Bacon.

Hall, N. (1987). *The emergence of literacy.* Portsmouth, NH: Heinemann.

Routman, R. (1988). *Transitions: From literature to literacy.* Portsmouth, NH: Heinemann.

Rudman, M.K., & Pierce, A.M. (1988). *For the love of reading: A parent's guide to encouraging young readers from infancy through age 5.* Mount Vernon, NY: Consumers Report Books.

Safford, P.L. (1989). *Integrated teaching in early childhood.* NY: Longman, Inc.

Sainto, D.M., & Lyon, S.R. (1989). Promoting successful mainstreaming transitions for handicapped preschool children. *Journal of Early Intervention,* 13 (4), 305-314.

Salend, S., & Moe L. (1983). Modifying nonhandicapped students' attitudes toward their handicapped peers through children's literature. *Journal of Special Educators,* 19 (3), 22-28.

Sawyer, S., & Comer, D.E. (1991). *Growing up with literature.* NY: Delmar.

Shrank, F.A., & Engles, D.W. (1981). Bibliotherapy as counseling adjunct: Research findings. *Personnel and Guidance Journal,* 60, 143-147.

Stephens, K. (1994). What is whole language? *First Teacher,* 15 (1), 6-7.

Notes

CHAPTER TWO

Using Books with Young Children

Introduction

Reading books to young children has a number of benefits that have been identified throughout the years. Children learn about their world and try to make sense of it through the books they read. In addition, they learn about themselves and develop positive attitudes about many things they have learned about through literature. This includes learning about the variety of people in our world and through this learning developing an understanding and sensitivity toward differences. Another benefit which is documented in the literature is that children develop an interest in reading and tend to be better readers when they have been read to consistently beginning at a young age (Sawyer & Comer, 1991).

It's important to have frequent and regular times for reading with young children. This should be a special time for the child to receive the undivided attention of a caring adult. Comfortably seated next to you, the story is shared. One of the ways that children learn to like reading is to associate these pleasurable times and feelings with reading (Jalongo, 1990).

The best way parents and teachers can help children become better readers is to read to them when they are very young. Children who are read to regularly grow up with the idea that reading is a normal part of daily life. As language becomes more meaningful, reading can stimulate imaginations and provide a foundation for new knowledge (Sawyer & Comer, 1991). According to Snyder (1991), children benefit the most from reading when they learn to identify words and letters, talk about the meaning of words, and when they discuss stories, he recommends friendly questions such as "What might happen next?" He cautions against interrogation about the story.

       Children should be read to on a daily basis. Sawyer and Comer (1991) stressed, "Each month that books are not read to infants is a month that is lost forever" (p. 17). There is no magic number of stories to be read daily but, the more, the better (Beaty, 1994). Books should always be available for children to use independently both at home and in school.

Reading to Infants

According to Schickendanz (1986), a four step approach is recommended when reading to infants:

1. Get the baby's attention or focus the baby's attention on a picture in the book. You might say, "Look!" or "Look at that!"
2. Ask the baby a labeling question such as, "What's that?"

3. Wait for the baby to respond, or when necessary, provide the answer yourself. The baby or adult answers by providing a label for the pictures.
4. Provide feedback to the baby. When the child is able to label the picture, provide feedback such as "Yes." or "You're right." If the label is difficult to understand, the adult should repeat the label. If the child labels the picture incorrectly, the adult should label it correctly such as "It looks like a little dog, but it's a cat."

Parents lead the dialogue because of the infant's limited language. Infants like the sounds of a caring voice and the rhythm of the language. As children get older and are able to participate more and more, the adult should allow them to take the lead. The attitude of the person reading the book influences the child. Books should be treated with respect and as something very special. With training and modeling, children will slowly learn how they should treat books (Sawyer & Comer, 1991).

Reading to Toddlers and Preschoolers

Toddlers like simple, colorful books and pictures and prefer to be close to an adult when reading. They also show an interest in books with predictable repetitions within the storyline. They like to join in with the familiar and predictable lines in addition to pointing and naming pictures. Toddlers are also ready for more sophisticated stories and rhymes. Preschoolers and kindergartners like a wider range of themes and are ready for more involved plots (Sawyer & Comer, 1991). They like to talk about the story after it is read. Children are able to talk about the story in a more meaningful way when parents and teachers use open-ended questions such as "What do you think about...?" "What would happened if...?" This encourages the children to think about the story not merely parrot back details of the story (Jalongo, 1990).

It can be expected that preschoolers will sit through short stories. However, infants and toddlers should be allowed to stop after just a few pages. Toddlers like to leave, roam around and then return to the person reading the story. They like to listen while in various positions and places; ideally, reading should take place on the floor (Sawyer & Comer, 1991). This level of attending is developmentally appropriate and should be anticipated and expected. A child's ability to attend steadily increases with age. To avoid frustration, it's important that our expectations for sitting and attending match the child's developmental stage.

Reading Aloud Effectively

It isn't necessary to be a professional storyteller in order to read stories to young children. While reading aloud does not come naturally to some people, anyone can practice and become an effective reader. Be sure to read books that you enjoy and you know the children will like. The reader's enthusiasm is contagious to the listeners. It's important that you become familiar with the books that you plan to read aloud. Reading books ahead of time makes it possible to become aware of parts of the story that may need to be shortened or explained further. Practice also gives you time to think about how you want to use your voice. If you are very unsure of reading aloud to children, the best way to learn is by listening to someone else read. Listen to how they use their voice and facial expressions. Observe how they interact with the children as they read the story. Read the book to yourself and think of how you want to sound. Read books over and over to children. They love them more each time they are read (Dilks, 1992).

Practice using a variety of voice inflections and volume levels. The rate of reading is also important. Reading slowly allows children to think about what is going to happen next. They can use their imaginations and form visual images. Speeding up when the action picks up can make it so exciting that the children can hardly wait to find out what will happen. But, be careful not to read too fast, a common mistake when reading aloud. Pausing at appropriate times can also be extremely effectively in helping to set the mood or tone of the story.

Remember that your voice is an important tool to be used when reading to children. Use your voice to differentiate between characters and to emphasize important parts of the story. Be careful not to get too carried away. The object is to read the book not to perform the story! Subtle changes in your voice can be very effective without getting overly dramatic. Practice reading the book so you are prepared to use your voice effectively (Jalongo, 1990).

The way the reader holds the book when reading to young children is very important in maintaining their interest. When reading to a group of children, the book should be held facing the group and at their eye level. With a group, the book needs to be moved slowly from side to side to make sure that all of the children see the words and illustrations. This movement can occur during or after reading each page. This may be difficult at first but will become easier with practice. With the book held in this manner, it's important that the reader is familiar with the story. When children are sitting on the reader's lap or next to the reader, the book is held in front of the group with the thumb in the center of the pages. With this type of grouping, the children will be able to see without moving the book from side to side (Sawyer & Comer, 1991). Children will become restless and frustrated if they cannot see the words and illustrations. Next, they will lose interest in the story. Planning and practice can keep this from happening and ensure that story time is a fun learning experience.

Additional Hints for Reading to Young Children

- Make it fun. Show enthusiasm when you read; never turn reading into a chore.
- Try to read every day. Make it part of your daily schedule; make it a priority.
- Begin reading to children when they are infants; the sooner, the better.
- Use rhymes to stimulate the infant's language and listening.
- Select simple, brightly colored pictures as they arouse children's curiosity.
- Read to children in a comfortable area using plenty of softness such as pillows.

- Let the child hold the book and turn the pages when appropriate.
- Pause between pages so the children can enjoy the illustrations.
- Point to the pictures as you talk about them.
- Point to the words you read; Children learn the black marks tell you what to say.
- When reading a familiar book, leave out words for the children to fill in.
- Make deliberate mistakes as you read so the children can "catch you."
- Whenever possible, add props to the story (e.g. stuffed animal, hats).
- When the children want the book read again and again, read it again!

(Miller, 1984; Threlease, 1989)

References

Beaty, J.J. (1994). *Picture book storytelling*. New York: Harcourt Brace College Publishers.

Dilks, C. (1992). *Creating a classroom literacy environment*. Philadelphia, PA: Children's Literacy Initiative.

Jalongo, M. R. (1990). *Young children and picture books*. Washington, DC: NAEYC.

Miller, K. M. (1984). *More things to do with toddlers and twos*. Chelsea, MA: Telshare Publishing, Inc.

Sawyer, W., & Comer, D. E. (1991). *Growing up with literature*. Delmar Publishers.

Schickedanz, J. A. (1986). *More than the ABCs*. Washington, DC: NAEYC.

Snyder, G. (1991). Parents, teachers, children and whole language. In V. Froese (Ed.), *Whole-language: Practice and theory* (pp. 255-281). Boston, MA: Allyn and Bacon.

Threlease, J. (1995). *The new read-aloud handbook (3rd ed.)*. New York: Penguin Books.

••••••••••••••

CHAPTER THREE

Teaching About Differences

Introduction

The books in this bibliography can be used to help teach and promote discussion about differences in the world. Besides using these books to teach about similarities and differences, each annotation identifies additional themes where these books can be incorporated. A variety of differences are included such as differences in the way people look, the clothes we wear, the foods we eat, the houses we live in, and the transportation we use. It can be fun learning about differences in ourselves, our families and others. It's important to introduce the concept of different in a positive way. Help children see that it's natural to have differences in our lives. This helps promote the development of a positive self-image. We must all be reminded that it's the differences in our world that make it an exciting place to live. Help children celebrate differences!

Children's Awareness of Differences

Children become aware of differences at a very early age. As young as toddlers, children learn to name physical characteristics such as skin and hair color. They notice location of body parts. It is at this age that they might develop fear or discomfort around unfamiliar attributes such as glasses, facial hair, skin color, and disabilities. Children who are three or four years of age base their thinking on how something looks, not on logic. Their thinking is limited and often distorted and inconsistent. This makes them very susceptible to believing in stereotypes. It is through the development of self-concept and self-esteem play that they learn to recognize and accept others. As intellectual development occurs during the preschool years, children develop the ability to see likenesses and differences. From this develops the awareness of how people are alike and different. Preschoolers are unable to understand that the inside of a person stays the same even though the physical appearance may change (York, 1991).

Derman-Sparks (1989) reminds us not to deny differences that children point out by saying, "She's just like you." Help children recognize how they are different and alike. In addition, don't criticize children for asking questions about differences with comments such as, "It isn't nice to look." This may teach children not to ask questions which can lead to misconceptions and fears.

How We Are Alike, Yet Different

When teaching children about likenesses and differences, be careful not to give the child any negative messages about differences. Begin with familiar things in their environment such as hair color, height and shoe size. While it's important to show how we are all the same (i.e. everyone has hair) it's just as important to show how we are different (i.e. my hair is brown, yours is blonde). While we may be different on the outside, children need to learn that we are alike on the inside with similar wants (we all want friends), needs (we all need food and drink), and feelings (we all get sad when we're teased).

Begin working on likenesses and differences that are concrete and the children can see such as hair or skin color. Later, move to those that are more abstract. When an idea is abstract, such as feelings, try to make it more concrete by focusing on what the child can see. What do people do when they are happy? Smile or laugh. What do people do when they are sad? Cry. Smiling, laughing and crying are concrete behaviors children can see which makes the abstract notion of feelings become more concrete and more easily understood.

We must discuss similarities as well as differences as this is how children are able to discover ways they are alike which helps build relationships. People can be alike yet different in many ways. Some of those that you can share with children are differences in people's appearance (i.e. My eyes are blue; your eyes are brown), feelings (i.e. I'm smiling because I am happy; she's crying because she is sad), abilities (i.e. I can ride my bike; you can print your name), homes (i.e. I live in an apartment; you live in a house), families (i.e. I have a family of five; you have three in your family), occupations (i.e. My mom's a police officer; your mom is a cashier at the supermarket). You will be able to think of many more ways people are alike and different. Talking about differences such as these lead into learning about differences in hearing, seeing, moving and other disabilities or illnesses. Differences about ourselves and our families are easier to understand and will lay the groundwork for understanding other types of differences which children will encounter throughout their lives.

Annotated Bibliography: Children's Books About Differences

Badt, Karin Luisa. *Hair There and Everywhere*, illus. and photographs by a variety of people. Children's Press, 1994. ISBN 0-516-48187-8 [32 p]. Nonfiction, Gr. 1-5.

The entire book is about hair! Included is some interesting history and hair styles from many different cultures and religions. The photographs and sketches are very interesting with the text appropriate for children third grade and up. Younger children would enjoy the photographs. A wonderful book to use to talk about differences - we all have hair but there are many differences in how it is groomed and how it looks!

Themes or Units: Body Awareness; Children and Families Around the World; We Are Alike, We Are Different.

Baer, Edith. *This is the Way We Go to School*, illus. by Steve Bjorkman. Scholastic, 1990. ISBN 0-590-43162-5 [36 p]. Nonfiction, Gr. PS-3.

This is a delightful book that shows children from around the world and the many different ways they travel to school. For example some children ride the cable cars, others ride bicycles, trains, and even helicopters. The illustrations will capture the children's excitement and incorporate diversity.

Themes or Units: Children and Families Around the World; Friends and School; Transportation.

Brown, Marc. *Arthur's Eyes*, illus. by author. Little, 1979. ISBN 0-316-11063-9 [30 p]. Fiction, Gr. PS-3.

This is a story about Arthur who has trouble seeing the blackboard at school and making baskets in gym class. The doctor tells Arthur he needs glasses. When Arthur wears his glasses to school his classmates tease him so he refuses to wear them. Then he discovers that the principal wears glasses too. This is an entertaining story with a predictable ending about the adjustment of wearing glasses.

Themes or Units: Feelings; Friends and School; Health; Sight (seeing); We Are Alike, We Are Different.

Cheltenham Elementary School Kindergartners. *We Are Alike...We Are All Different*, illus. by authors, photographs by Laura Dwight. Scholastic, 1991. ISBN 0-590-49173-3 [27 p]. Nonfiction, Gr. PS-2.

This book was created by a kindergarten class to help children learn about diversity. They explored likenesses and differences among themselves. The children with the help of their teacher wrote the text and drew the illustrations; photographs were added. This book won the Cabbage Patch Kids/Scholastic "We Are Different...We Are Alike" Creative Teacher Awards Program. This is an excellent beginning book to talk about differences of all kinds.

Themes or Units: Families; Friends and School; We Are Alike, We Are Different.

de Poix, Carol. *Jo, Flo and Yolanda,* **illus. by Stephanie Sove Ney. Lollipop Power, Inc., 1973. ISBN 0-914996-04-5 [32 p]. Fiction, Gr. PS-3.**

Jo, Flo and Yolanda are triplets. This story points out all of the ways they are alike and different. Jo likes to read and wants to explore and write. Flo likes to play baseball and wants to be a baseball player. Yolanda likes to cook and wants to have her own restaurant. This story points out that while we have similarities, we all have differences too, even when you are triplets! Cultural diversity is noted in the illustrations and Spanish translation is provided.

Themes or Units: **Brothers & Sisters; City; Families; We Are Alike, We Are Different.**

Dorros, Arthur. *This is My House,* **illus. by author. Scholastic, Inc., 1992. ISBN 0-590-45303-3 [30 p]. Nonfiction, Gr. PS-2.**

This book shows the many different kinds of houses people live in around the world. "This is my house" is printed under the illustration of each house in the language of the country where the house is located. Nineteen countries are represented with a variety of houses from a highrise apartment building in Hong Kong to a houseboat in Thailand. People are all the same in that they all have houses, but they are also different by the kind of houses in which they live.

Themes or Units: **Buildings; Children and Families Around the World; Homes and Neighborhoods; We Are Alike, We Are Different.**

Hamanaka, Sheila. *All The Colors of The Earth,* **illus. by author. Morrow Junior Books, 1994. ISBN 0-688-11131-9 [30 p]. Fiction, Gr. PS-3. Differences.**

Superb illustrations show children from many cultures; the ways children are alike and different. It points out that people come in many different colors and hues. The book has limited text with outstanding illustrations in warm colors that really tell the story.

Themes or Units: **Body Awareness; Children & Families Around the World; Colors in My World; We Are Alike, We Are Different.**

Holy Cross School Kindergartners. *What's Under Your Hood, Orson?,* **illus. by Terry Kovalcik. Scholastic, 1993. ISBN 0-590-49247-0 [28 p]. Fiction, Gr. PS-1.**

This book was written by a kindergarten class in New York and was a winner in the Scholastic Contest. The story is about two cars, Yellow and Blue, who are friends. Along comes Red who wants to be a friend. Blue and Yellow come to realize that Red might look different, but under the hood they are all alike. They wonder if people are the same way. This story points out there can be external differences yet internal similarities.

Themes or Units: **Colors in My World (red, blue, yellow); Friendship; Transportation; We Are Alike, We Are Different.**

Leventhal, Debra. *What Is Your Language?*, illus. by Monica Wellington. **Dutton, 1994. ISBN 0-525-45133-1 [32 p]. Fiction, Gr. PS-3.**
As a young boy visits countries around the world he asks, "What is your language? Please tell me now." Children from each country answer him and demonstrate how they say "yes" in each of their languages. The text is an easy-to-learn song that children enjoy singing as they learn about cultural similarities and differences.
Themes or Units: **Children and Families Around the World; We Are Alike, We Are Different.**

Macdonald, Maryann. *Little Hippo Gets Glasses*, pictures by Anna King. **Dial Books, 1991. ISBN 0-8037-0964-1 [24 p]. Fiction, Gr. K-2.**
Children often perceive themselves as being different when they need to wear glasses. This was the case with Little Hippo who needed glasses to see television and the blackboard at school. He feels better about wearing glasses when he finds that Sophia needs glasses too. A delightful book that may help children feel better about wearing their glasses. The anthropomorphic approach is very effective.
Themes or Units: **Dentists, Doctors, Nurses & Hospitals; Feelings; Friends & School; Friendship; Health; Safety; Sight (seeing); We Are Alike, We Are Different.**

McDonald, Megan. *The Potato Man*, illus. by Ted Lewin. **Orchard, 1991. ISBN 0-531-08514-7 [32 p]. Fiction, Gr. PS-2.**
Potato Man would come to town selling vegetables. They called him Potato Man because he had only one eye with skin lumpy as a potato. The children were afraid of him but it was just old Mr. Angelo who had lost his eye in the war. This is an outstanding story that could promote good discussion about fears children might have when someone looks different. The colored illustrations do an outstanding job of representing life in the early 1900's.
Themes or Units: **Feelings; Giving and Sharing; Grandmothers and Grandfathers; Holidays Around the World (Christmas); We Are Alike, We Are Different.**

Morris, Ann. *Bread Bread Bread*, photographs by Ken Heyman. **Scholastic, 1989. ISBN 0-590-46036-6 [29 p]. Nonfiction, Gr. PS-2.**
Colorful photographs show the many varieties of bread that are eaten by people throughout the world. The shape, texture, and how it's made may be different, but it is all bread. Bread is also toasted in different ways - from a fancy toaster to an open fire.
Themes or Units: **Foods in My World; Shapes, Sizes, & Weights; We Are Alike, We Are Different.**

Morris, Ann. *Hats Hats Hats,* **photographs by Ken Heyman. Scholastic, 1989. ISBN 0-590-44878-1 [29 p]. Nonfiction, Gr. PS-2.**
People around the world model many kinds of hats all captured in beautiful colored photographs. Included are fun hats, work hats, play hats, warm hats and much more. All people wear hats, but a variety of hats are worn in different parts of the world.
Themes or Units: **Children and Families Around the World; Hats; We Are Alike, We Are Different.**

Morris, Ann. *On The Go,* **photographs by Ken Heyman. Scholastic, 1990. ISBN 0-590-45995-3 [29 p]. Nonfiction, Gr. PS-3.**
This book shows the many different kinds of transportation are used in different parts of the world. Colorful photographs show a variety of vehicles. The story begins with people transporting goods, then the goods are transported by vehicles with wheels that are pushed or pulled by people. Finally, there are vehicles that are fueled to run by themselves.
Themes or Units: **Transportation; We Are Alike, We Are Different; Wheels.**

Nikola-Lisa, W. *Bein' With You This Way,* **illus. by Michael Bryant. Lee & Low Books, 1994. ISBN 1-880000-05-9**
[27 p]. Fiction, Gr. PS-3.
As a group of children play at the part, they discover that despite their physical differences such as straight hair, curly hair; brown eyes, blue eyes; light skin, dark skin; they are all really the same. The narrative is written in an entertaining verse which the author refers to as "playground rap." Illustrations show the diversity of children all having fun together. An entertaining book that points out differences in a way that shows the reader that differences are okay.
Themes or Units: **Body Awareness; Friendship; Homes & Neighborhoods; Summer; We Are Alike, We Are Different.**

Quinsey, Mary Beth. *Why Does That Man Have Such A Big Nose?,* **illus. by author. Parenting Press, 1983.**
ISBN 0-943-990-25-4 [32 p]. Fiction, PS-3.
This book answers questions innocently asked by children about people who children see as different. The photographs show a variety of differences in people's appearance including size, choice of clothing, skin color, disability, and facial features. The text provides responses to each question while helping the child empathize with the person. This is an amusing book and would be an excellent choice when teaching about differences.
Themes or Units: **Body Awareness; Feelings; We Are Alike, We Are Different.**

Simon, Norma. *All Kinds of Families*, **illus. by Joe Lasker. Albert Whitman & Co., 1976. ISBN 0-8075-0282-0 [34 p]. Fiction, PS-3.**
This story reflects the many patterns of family life and illustrates the family as parents and children, whether living together or not. The story stresses the supportive function of the family and emphasizes the child being in the center of the system. The book is realistic in that it also shows in a very sensitive way that some families are troubled. Cultural diversity is incorporated in the families presented.
Themes or Units: **Children and Families Around the World; Families; Grandmothers and Grandfathers; We Are Alike, We Are Different.**

Simon, Norma. *Why Am I Different?*, **pictures by Dora Leder. Albert Whitman, 1976. ISBN 0-8075-90-74-6**
[31 p]. Fiction, PS-3.
A number of concepts are introduced which lead to a positive view of differences that are attributed to growth, preferences and abilities which are shaped by our home and neighborhood experiences, family standards, and ethnic, cultural, and religious backgrounds. Self-respect and respect for others is emphasized. The illustrations depict cultural diversity.
Themes or Units: **Families; Feelings; Friendship; Homes & Neighborhoods; We Are Alike, We Are Different.**

Spier, Peter. *People*, **illus. by author. Delacorte Press, 1980. ISBN 0-385-13181-X [38 p]. Fiction, All Ages.**
This book is about the many people who live in the world. With few words and many pictures, it points out differences in how people look, dress, where people live, the languages they speak and write and much, much more. This book is for all ages. It's a book that needs to be looked at many times because of all the pictures. The story ends by illustrating how boring the world would be if everyone would look, think, eat, dress and act the same.
Themes or Units: **Body Awareness; Buildings; Children and Families Around the World; Clothing; Foods in My World; Hats; Homes and Neighborhoods; Pet Animals; We Are Alike, We Are Different.**

Takeshita, Fumiko. *The Park Bench*, **illus. by Mamoru Suzuki. Kane/Miller Book Publishers, 1989.**
ISBN 0-916291-21-9 [32 p]. Fiction, Gr. K-2.
This book was originally published in Japan. The narrative is provided in both English and Japanese. The story is about "a day in the life of a park bench." The reader is introduced to all of the different people that use the park bench including a grandpa, mothers, children, and friends; and, all of the different reasons they use the bench, i.e. to meet friends, to rest and to sit in the sunlight. This story provides another way of looking at differences.
Themes or Units: City; **Community Helpers (park worker); Summer.**

References

Byrnes, D. A., & Kiger, G. (Eds.). (1992). *Common bonds: Anti-bias teaching in a diverse society.* Wheaton, MD: Association for Childhood Education International.

Froschl, M., Colon, L., Rubin, E., & Sprung, B. (1984). *Including all of us: An early childhood curriculum about disability.* New York: Educational Equity Concepts, Inc.

Derman-Sparks, L. (1989). *Anti-bias curriculum.* Washington, DC: NAEYC.

York, S. (1991). *Roots & wings.* Mpls., MN: Redleaf Press.

· · · · · · · · · · · · ·
CHAPTER FOUR

Teaching About Disabilities and Chronic Illness to Young Children

Introduction

When presenting information about disabilities or illness to young children it's important to be open and honest. It's best to answer their questions when they are asked using simple, respectful language while providing clear, accurate information. Providing information about disabilities is much like teaching young children about sex! Give enough information to answer their questions but not enough to overwhelm them. By being aware of the child's age and developmental level, you can present information in a way that the child will be able to understand. Use accurate terminology. Children can learn what terms mean if you introduce new words slowly. With information such as this, you will be establishing a base of knowledge which can be built upon throughout the upcoming weeks, months, and years.

Encouraging and answering questions is the most natural way for children to learn. This openness will help them feel it's okay to ask questions. Remember, no question is a "dumb" question. Children should not be made to feel embarrassed about any questions they might ask. For example, a young child may want to know how someone in a wheelchair is able to go to the bathroom. Questions such as this reflect the natural curiosity of young children and should be answered openly and honestly. As children get older their questions will become more complex since they will have developed a greater level of understanding. Your answers will need to reflect this change in development by providing more in-depth information.

Children often express fears about a disability or illness. Some common fears are that they will catch the disability or fear of the equipment. With honest information it's possible to dispel such fears. Children are sometimes confused about what a child with a particular disability can and cannot do. It's difficult for them to grasp what having a disability really means because they have not had first hand experience. It's important for children to see that with the use of aids (e.g. wheelchair, sign language) and adapting how to do things people with disabilities can do many of the activities they do even if it's done in a somewhat different way.

Remember, it's the unknown that frightens children. If they do not ask questions, parents and professionals should facilitate question asking and discussion. One way to do this is by reading stories that include someone with a disability or illness. In order to answer children's questions, parents and professionals need to have basic information about disabilities and illnesses. A brief overview of the disabilities and chronic illnesses that are represented in this selection of children's literature is provided in this chapter.

Spiraling Concepts Throughout The Curriculum or Throughout Time

Learning about disabilities or illness is not a one time event. Information should be spiraled throughout the curriculum or throughout time to enhance learning. This means that information about a disability or illness is introduced to children with time for discussion and ample opportunity to have questions answered. In the future, the parent or professional talks about the disability or illness when another opportunity naturally occurs. The child may ask a question, or you may see something in the newspaper or on television that sparks a conversation. Using these teachable moments you then talk about the disability or illness or related issues building on the information previously provided to the children. In the event opportunities such as these do not occur, the parent or professional should periodically re-introduce the topic in order to create the opportunity for further discussion. In early childhood and primary programs, disability and illness should become part of the ongoing curriculum, not a one week unit during "Disability Awareness Week" which we know is not effective for optimal learning.

Respect and Dignity

Respect means that you talk about and interact with children with disabilities or illness much like you would any other child. Professionals and parents can demonstrate this respect in their behaviors toward the child. For example, be a good listener to a child whose speech comes slowly; allow children to become independent by assisting them with tasks only when it's needed.

Sometimes it is necessary to teach children to be respectful of those who are different from themselves. Rejection might happen for a number of reasons such as fear, anxiety, impatience, stereotyping or lack of skills for interacting with the child with the disability (Derman-Sparks, 1989). It may be that they don't know how to act or don't understand what is expected of them. If children use name-calling or demonstrate any other inappropriate behavior (make faces) interrupt their language or behavior and through modeling and verbalizing show them appropriate ways to interact. Teaching children how to be respectful of others is most effectively done through positive modeling. When children see their teachers and parents modeling respectful behaviors, they will begin to imitate these same behaviors.

Being respectful means the professional or parent does not talk about the disability to another adult or child in front of the child with the disability. Sometimes adults do this because they forget or think the child can't hear or won't understand what they are saying. Sometimes a child doesn't understand all that is being said, but may understand some words and pick up on the tone of the conversation. It's also possible that children understand more than you think. Even very young children can tell when people are talking about them. Talking in front of the children demonstrates a lack of respect for them as people. A more respectful strategy would be to step into the hall or another room to discuss or share information.

When telling someone about the disability, the child can be invited to help explain if he or she is capable and if the child wants to participate. For example, what better way to understand what it's like to be in a wheelchair all day than to ask the person who does it. It's very important that children are invited to participate. This gives them the opportunity to participate if they feel comfortable and decline if they feel uncomfortable. Participating should be their choice and whatever choice they make should be acceptable.

When talking to individuals with disabilities, it's important to remember that it is not necessary to speak loudly to them. Sometimes when a child or adult with a disability does not seem to understand what is being said, people talk more loudly to them. Increasing the intensity of your voice does not increase the person's ability to understand. Again, this behavior lacks respect. Instead, it would be helpful if you simplify some of your words or shorten your sentences in an effort to help them understand. Be careful not to talk down to someone who has the capabilities of understanding you. If you are not sure, ask the person, "Do you understand?" Most often they will be able to tell you. This demonstrates respect.

Using "Person First" Language

"The words or phrases people speak and write plus the order in which they are sequenced greatly affects the images that are formed about individuals with disabilities and the negative or positive impressions that result" (Blaska, 1993, p. 25). To demonstrate respect when talking about individuals with disabilities, use "person first" language. "Person first" means that you refer to people first as individuals and then to their disability when this referent is needed using words that are descriptive yet respectful. If you use "person first" language when you talk to young children about people with disabilities, they will learn to use appropriate words by modeling your language. This will help eliminate stereotypic language.

Use this:	Instead of This:
Child with a disability	Disabled child
Child with Down syndrome	Down syndrome child
Child with retardation	Retarded child
Boy with a physical disability	Crippled Boy
Person with epilepsy	Epileptic

To keep this philosophy in perspective, think about how you might introduce a friend who does not have a disability. You would first use that person's name and then tell where he or she works or lives or whatever. Should it be any different for someone with a disability? Everyone is made up of many characteristics and most people don't care to be identified by only one of them (PACER, 1989).

The "person first" philosophy was first adopted by (TASH) The Association for Persons with Severe Handicaps (Bailey, 1992). Many advocacy organizations and disability groups have published similar information to educate the public. Perske (1988) tells about a woman who stood up at a meeting and said, "We are tired of being seen first as handicapped, or retarded, or developmentally disabled. We want to be seen as people first" (p. 5). When we use the expression "the deaf child" it makes the disability the most important characteristic about the child, while saying, "the child who is deaf" takes the focus away from the disability, making it but one of the descriptors. This order of reference is often more awkward, but it is more respectful of persons with disabilities (Blaska, 1993).

Examples of "Person First" Language

Disability vs Handicapped

There has been much debate whether to use "disability" or "handicap." Generally, a disability is defined as a condition of the person which might be emotional or physical. While a handicap is the result of environmental or societal barriers (Hadley & Brodwin, 1988). In reality, a disability does not have to be a handicap. A disability may mean "that a person may do something a little bit differently from a person who does not have a disability, but with equal participation and equal results" (Kailes, 1985, p. 68).

Use This:	Instead of This:
The boy with a disability	The handicapped boy
Children with disabilities	Handicapped children
Children without disabilities	Nonhandicapped children
Disabling conditions	Handicapping conditions

Normal vs Abnormal

The problem with using the term "normal" when referring to a person without a disability is the inference that a person with a disability is "abnormal" or "not normal." A person with a disability may have some abnormal development, but he or she is not an "abnormal" person. When using terms such as these, it's important that you are talking or writing about development and not about a person or program (Blaska, 1993).

Use This:	Instead of This:
Normal development	Normal child
Child without a disability	Normal child
Mainstream classroom	Normal classroom
Children without disabilities	Normal children or normal peers

Words To Avoid

There are a number of words that should be avoided because they have a negative or judgemental connotation (Tyler, 1990). Words such as these do not demonstrate respect and fail to recognize the person's strengths and abilities. They create images of people who are to be pitied and perpetuate negative stereotypes of people with disabilities.

Avoid using works such as:

Victim	Disease
Suffers from	Unfortunate
Stricken	Poor
Crippled	Drain or burden
Afflicted	Confined.

Categorizing People

People with disabilities should not be grouped into categories such as "the retarded" or "the handicapped" (Hanft, 1989). Do we view all children with Down syndrome as happy and friendly who will never be able to read? Or, do we see children as individuals with their own strengths and limitations?

Use This:	Instead of This:
People with disabilities	The disabled or the handicapped
People with retardation	The retarded
Children with visual impairments who are blind	The blind

Additional Suggestions

Using the verb "to have." The most effective way of expressing the link between a person and a disability is to use a form of the verb "to have" (Hadley & Brodwin, 1988). Tyler (1990) says, "A person is a human being and should not be confused with a condition" (p. 65). We should say "the child has autism" instead of "is autistic." "The child has mental retardation" instead of "is retarded." "The child has spastic muscles" instead of "is spastic."

Disability or disease. A disability is not a disease. People with disabilities are often very healthy. Words such as symptoms, cases or patients should be avoided unless talking or writing about someone's health or medical condition.

Portrayal. People with disabilities should "be portrayed as actively going about the business of living as other people do, *not* as passive victims, tragic figures or "super-heroes" (Hadley & Brodwin, 1988).

Special. "Special" is a word that is routinely used when referring to persons with disabilities. Pershe (1988) shed some light on using this term, "Being seen as special might not be so bad, if you're a top celebrity or the national champion. But, if you've been singled out as not normal, given a label, excluded from full participation, exist in out of the way residences, or attend "out of the real world programs" when you felt you wanted to live "in the middle of things," calling you special might only add to the wound you already feel" (p. 59). All persons with disabilities may not be offended by using the term "special." However, let Pershe's comments serve as a reminder to all of us to choose our words carefully and always speak with respect to all people (Blaska, 1993).

Overview of Disabilities
and Chronic Illnesses
With Responses to Children's Questions

Autism or Autistic Like Behavior

Autism is a disorder of the brain which causes severe impairment of the way sensory input is assimilated into the brain (Milota, et al., 1991). It is a serious brain-based developmental disability. The major characteristics are a global language disorder, abnormal behavior patterns, social isolation and, most often, mental retardation (Batshaw & Perret, 1992). Autism differs from mental retardation in that the characteristic feature of autism is not a developmental delay, rather it's a series of deviations from normal development that is apparent by age three. Behaviors often noted with these children include sing-song, monotonous speech (for those who have language), parroting or repeating words or phrases (echolalia), a limited behavioral repertoire, lack of tolerance to environmental change, self-stimulating behaviors (e.g. hand flapping), self-abusive behaviors and obsessive rituals and routines (Batshaw & Perret, 1992).

According to Powers (1989) there are five major symptoms of autism: 1) Failure to develop normal socialization which is the most noticeable symptom of autism. They don't interact the way most children do or may not interact at all often preferring to be alone most of the time. There is a lack of interest in the thoughts and feelings of others and an absence of eye contact, 2) Disturbances in speech, language, and communication which is the second major symptom. Forty percent do not speak at all and others rely excessively on jargon, use words or phrases out of context or use echolalia which is a parrot like repetition of what has just been said, 3) Abnormal relationships to objects and events which describes their inability to relate normally to things or events and causes their play to be very unusual. They may not play at all or may use toys in unusual ways. They have impaired social imagination which refers to an inability to imitate, engage in pretend play or imagine someone else's thoughts and feelings. Additional social deficits include not seeking comfort when hurt and a lack of interest in friendships, 4) Abnormal responses to sensory stimulation which refers to their responses to things in the environment that we hear, see, feel, smell, and touch. These children may overreact or not react at all to various stimuli. Oversensitivity is very common, and 5) Developmental delays or differences refer to the significantly different ways in which children with autism develop. Their development is very uneven with communication, social, and cognition delayed while motor may be relatively normal or only slightly delayed. Their sequence of learning may also be very different. Onset of the symptoms of autism is usually before 2 1/2 years of age with the characteristics becoming more pronounced around 3-4 years (Peterson, 1987).

Like many other disabilities, there seems to be a range of autistic behaviors that are displayed. When children have severe behaviors they are referred to as being **autistic**. These children are almost always non-verbal. Those with moderate behaviors or characteristics have differences in the way they interact verbally and socially and are referred to as being **autistic-like** or having **pervasive developmental disorder (PDD)**. Children with mild characteristics often resemble someone with a severe learning disability (Milota, et al., 1991). Therapy for children with autism is interdisciplinary including psychiatry, speech-language therapy, behavior management, and social work to provide assistance to the family.

Children may ask about the unusual behaviors particularly any self-stimulating or abusive patterns or the child's inability to communicate. Answer simply and honestly such as: "He likes the movement of his hands as they flap, but he's working on remembering not to do that." "She has a hard time understanding what she sees or hears because her brain works differently than yours and mine." "Learning to talk has been hard for Suzy, but she is learning some new words. We need to learn her sign language too. Remember, there are different ways to communicate and that's okay!" Your answers should always be honest while respectful and positive.

Blind or Partially Sighted

A child who has a visual disability has a visual impairment which, even with correction, adversely affects a child's educational performance (Federal Register, 1977). These children are unable to use their vision to learn in the same way that children with normal vision use their sight to learn.

When talking about low vision or blindness, the concern lies in **visual acuity** which is the ability to see something at a specified distance. Visual acuity is measured by having the person discriminate objects or read letters at a distance of 20 feet. This is most often done with the Snellen Chart. Visual acuity is then expressed as a fraction or ratio which tells how well the person can see. For example, the expression 20/20 which is familiar to most people means that the person reads letters or discriminates objects at 20 feet that a person with normal vision can read or discriminate at 20 feet. The ratio 20/90 means that the person can read or discriminate at 20 feet what a person with normal vision can read or discriminate at 90 feet, etc. (Deiner, 1993).

Having low vision or being **partially sighted** refers to a loss of visual acuity in the range of 20/70 to 20/200 with correction. The American Federation for the Blind prefers using the term partially sighted to identify children with some degree of visual impairment. These children have enough usable vision to learn with the help of magnifiers and large print books (Deiner, 1993).

Being **blind** refers to children who have no vision or have only light perception. Being legally blind means having visual acuity in both eyes of less than 20/200 after the best correction with glasses. Many children who are identified as legally blind have light perception which means they are still able to distinguish between varying shades of light (Batshaw & Perret, 1992). Children who are blind need to rely on their senses of touch and hearing in order to learn. Aids used by this group include Braille, guide dogs or white canes, talking books, computers, as well as other forms of technology.

The most common congenital causes of blindness or partial sightedness in children are intrauterine infections, such as German measles, and malformations. Other causes are retinopathy of prematurity, head trauma, anoxic events, tumors, and eye infections (Batshaw & Perret, 1992). Retinopathy of Prematurity (ROP) is a disease of the retina where scar tissue forms behind the lens and develops a mass that causes detachment of the retina from the optic nerve. It usually occurs in both eyes and causes complete loss of sight. The major cause of this condition is the high concentration of oxygen which is needed to keep premature infants alive (Deiner, 1993; Milota et al., 1991).

Young children have difficulty understanding what it's like to be blind. Depending on their ages, these children may be unable or have limited ability to imagine being blind. For this reason, it's helpful to have children actively participate in concrete activities which makes the abstract notion of blindness become more real. See Appendix A for suggested activities.

Children will be naturally curious and have many questions. Answers might be: "She can't see because her eyes don't work like ours. The nerves behind her eyes don't work so she not able to see." "Her eyes are open but she sees darkness." "No, her eyes don't hurt." "No, you can't 'catch' being blind." "He can see but his eyes work differently than ours so it's hard for him to see things that are small or far away."

Chronic Illness or Health Impairments

Children who have chronic illnesses that will affect their learning are considered by federal law to have a health impairment. Public Law 102-119 Individuals with Disabilities Education Act (IDEA - formerly P.L. 94-142) describes "other health impaired" as having "limited strength, vitality or alertness, due to chronic or acute health problems such as heart condition, tuberculosis, rheumatic fever, nephritis, asthma, sickle cell anemia, hemophilia, epilepsy, lead poisoning, leukemia or diabetes, which adversely affects a child's educational performance" (Federal Register, 1977). Children with chronic illnesses that affect learning are entitled to all of the rights afforded students with disabilities according to special education law.

Acquired Immune Deficiency Syndrome (AIDS)

AIDS is a communicable viral disease that is life-threatening and has no known cure or vaccine. The human immunodeficiency virus (HIV) itself does not kill but it weakens the immune system making the body unable to defend itself against other diseases. **Acquired** means the disease is transmitted through direct contact with blood, semen, or breast milk. An infant may contract AIDS from its mother while in utero. **Immune** is the system of the body that is affected and **Deficiency** describes how the immune system is unable to fight off harmful organs that invade it. **Syndrome** refers to the group of symptoms that make up the disease (Batshaw & Perret, 1992; Deiner, 1993).

It is not always possible to know if any of the children with whom you work have AIDS, therefore, universal cleaning and disinfection procedures should be routinely used which includes appropriate handwashing, cleaning, and disposal of contaminated items (Epidemiology Departments, 1987). Good hygiene is important for everyone at home and in programs to help prevent the spread of infections.

In addition to chronic health needs, AIDS may also cause psychotic behavior, mental retardation, seizures, and neurological impairments (Hallahan & Kauffman, 1991). What to tell young children about AIDS is a difficult question. For children functioning under eight years of age, information about AIDS would probably be beyond their cognitive abilities and serve only to frighten them. Should a child ask a question, be sure to provide an honest yet simple answer. If a young child asks: "What is AIDS?" Your answer might be that it is a serious disease but he or she does not have to worry about catching it. Children need to feel safe at home and in school environments.

While an increasing number of children are contracting the disease through their mothers, it is in utero or through the birth process. Some researchers are predicting that as the numbers of children with HIV infection continues to grow, the virus will become the leading infectious cause of mental retardation and developmental disability in children (Hallahan & Kauffman, 1994).

Allergies

The most common health impairment in children is allergies. An allergy is a sensitivity to something in the environment that is harmless to most people. Four categories of allergic substances have been identified: airborne or inhalants (e.g. plant pollen), foods and drugs which are ingested, direct contact with the skin (e.g. soap), and some drugs and chemicals which are injected (e.g. penicillin) (Deiner, 1993).

It is possible that allergies can affect a child's development, ability to learn, behavior, and interpersonal relationships. One of the side effects of some medications is drowsiness and may effect the child's ability to concentrate. It's important to know if any of the children with whom you work have allergies. Find out from parents what the child is allergic to, his or her common reactions, what you should do, and if medication is administered, are there any side effects. Have emergency procedures in place for children who might have their first allergic reaction when they are with you (Deiner, 1993). Children may ask why a friend doesn't eat a particular food. An answer might be, "His body doesn't work like yours and mine and that food will make him sick if he eats it."

Asthma

Asthma is a respiratory problem caused by a swelling of the bronchial tubes or the membrane lining. This swelling causes an obstruction of the small bronchial tubes which can result in shortness of breath, coughing, or wheezing and choking. The most common cause of asthma is allergies. Attacks can be triggered by excitement, overexertion or even ordinary activity. Children with asthma usually have medication in pill or inhaler form to take when attacks occur. These children are frequently absent from school which may affect their rate of learning (Deiner, 1993). Other children may be curious about the inhalers that they see used. An answer that explains how the medicine in the inhaler helps the child breathe more easily will satisfy most children.

Cancer

Cancer is a term that describes a group of diseases that produce malignant tumors in some part of the body. It is usually treated with surgery, radiation, chemotherapy, or a combination of these methods. The most common form of cancer in young children is **leukemia** which is a disease of the tissues that produce the white blood cells. In persons with leukemia, an overabundance of white cells are produced that are not effective in fighting infection and disrupt red blood cell production and prevent blood from clotting properly. Once leukemia is diagnosed, intensive treatment is ordered, often followed by a period of remission when the child looks and acts healthy. Medications may take away the child's appetite. Good nutrition is very important at this time (Deiner, 1993). Loss of hair may frighten some children. Assurance that the hair will grow back is needed. The word cancer may be very scary to some children. It's important that they understand that there are many types of cancer and with some cancers people do get well and live full lives.

Diabetes

Diabetes is a metabolic disorder of the pancreas. **Insulin** is a hormone made by the pancreas and is needed to help the body use glucose. With diabetes, the pancreas is unable to produce enough insulin or the insulin being produced is ineffective. Because the pancreas is not working properly, excess fatty acids can poison the body. If this occurs and goes untreated, diabetic coma and death can occur. To prevent this from happening, insulin therapy can be initiated. While insulin can't cure diabetes, it can control the disease. To be successful, a proper balance is needed between the insulin and food sugar. A well-rounded diet free of sugar is needed in order to maintain this balance. Exercise is also very important because it helps the insulin work appropriately. Some adults can control their diabetes with diet, however children usually require insulin injections in order to control their disease (Milota, 1991).

Young children are generally unable to recognize the warning signs of an insulin reaction. The child may be dizzy, trembling, shaky, or might have an emotional outburst just before the insulin reaction (Deiner, 1993). Find out in advance what you should do if an insulin reaction should occur. Generally you should have some quick-burning sugar available to give to the child. The key is to be prepared ahead of time. Snacks and lunches should also be discussed with the parents to ensure the timing and content are appropriate for the child.

When children ask questions, explain how Suzy's body doesn't work like yours and mine and if she eats sweets like candy, she'll get very sick.

Epilepsy or Seizure Disorder

Epilepsy is a disorder of the brain and is not a disease. It is characterized by **seizures** which are abnormal discharges of electrical energy in certain brain cells (Deiner, 1993). During the time when these electrical charges are occurring, the seizures can cause a temporary loss of consciousness or some temporary changes in behavior, bodily functions, sensations, or motor activity (Milota et al., 1991; Reisner, 1988).

Seizures can take many forms, however there are two major types. **Generalized** seizures involve the entire body because the discharge of cells is in a large portion of the brain. Whereas, **partial** seizures involve only a small or localized part of the brain causing only a small part of the body to be involved. Seizures can last several minutes or for just a few seconds. Likewise, they can occur frequently or once a year. Some seizures can be totally controlled by medications while other types, only partially controlled. After a seizure occurs, the child will be tired and need an opportunity to rest (Hallahan & Kaufman, 1991). Persons working with children with seizures must have the necessary background information to understand what type of seizures they have, if the seizures are controlled by medication, what medication the child takes and any side effects. In addition, you need to know first aid procedures in the event a seizure does occur.

Seeing someone have a seizure can be scary to young children. Stay calm and answer their questions openly and honestly with as much information as they want and can understand. Responses might be: "Sometimes her brain gets extra energy and it causes her body to move around. When it's over she is tired and needs to rest." "No, it doesn't hurt." "No, it won't happen to you because your brain has a different amount of energy."

Deaf or Hearing Impaired

Deafness describes a severe hearing loss which prevents people from understanding speech through hearing alone. They must rely on visual methods such as lip-reading or sign language. **Hearing loss** or **hard of hearing** refers to a loss that is not severe enough to interfere with hearing as the primary modality for understanding speech and learning (Milota et al., 1991). A hearing loss occurs when part of the hearing structure is malformed or malfunctions. While this affects hearing, it also may hinder a child's speech and language development, especially if this damage occurs prior to two years of age (Batshaw & Perret, 1993).

Hearing is measured with special equipment that is administered by a trained audiologist. The hearing loss is expressed in terms of decibels (dBs). Degrees of hearing loss are determined by measuring the softest sound that can be heard at three different frequencies and than averaging these measurements (Bradshaw & Perret, 1993).

There are two types of hearing impairments classified according to their location in the hearing process: **Conductive loss** is when the outer or middle ear prevents sound from getting into the inner ear. This reduces the child's ability to hear speech sounds and is most often caused by an object lodged in the ear canal, excessive ear wax, or otitis media which is fluid in the ear. Most often this type of hearing loss can be corrected through surgery.
Sensorineural loss occurs when there is damage to either the inner ear, the nerve to the brain stem or both. This type of loss is usually congenital, caused

by high fevers or some medicines that are used. This type of loss cannot be treated surgically. A hearing aid is prescribed which makes sounds louder but they remain distorted and unclear to the child (Deiner, 1993).

One percent (1%) of all children have a persistent hearing loss. Of these losses, 40% are mild, 20% moderate, 20% severe, and 20% profound. A child with a **mild hearing loss** has trouble hearing distant sounds or soft speech. Their speech is usually normal. Those with a **moderate loss** have difficulty hearing even loud conversation. They usually have a limited vocabulary, errors in their speech and some abnormal voice quality.

Children with **severe hearing loss** hear loud environmental sounds but not words. If this loss has occurred prior to age two, their language and speech does not develop spontaneously, however speech can be taught with amplification. Children with a **profound hearing loss** may hear some loud environmental sounds but hearing will not be their primary modality for learning as they will not comprehend speech (Batshaw & Perret, 1993). The effect of hearing loss on the development of speech and language development depends on the severity of the loss, the age of onset, the age when the loss was discovered, and the age when the intervention occurs.

There are three main causes of deafness in infants: genetic, passed from the parents to the child, diseases such as German measles or meningitis, and trauma or injury (Meyer, Vadasy, & Fewell, 1985). However, the cause of hearing loss in many children remains unknown (Milota et al., 1991).

The causes of acquired hearing loss in children includes otitis media (middle ear infection), prenatal and postnatal infections, anoxia, prematurity, some antibiotics, and trauma. Ninety-five percent (95%) of all acquired hearing losses are due to middle ear infections (Batshaw & Perret, 1993).

Young children have a difficult time imagining what it would be like if you couldn't hear or if you could only hear some environmental sounds. Simulation activities can help them realize what it might be like. See Appendix A for suggested activities. Responses to children's questions might be: "He can't hear because his ears don't work like yours and mine." "The thing in his ear is part of his hearing aid. It makes sounds louder to help him hear us." "Jimmy isn't able to say many words so he 'talks' with his hands by signing," OR "He uses sign language because he isn't able to talk like you and I." "Because his ears don't work, he wasn't able to hear and learn to say the words people were using." "No, you can't catch it. Mindy was born this way," OR "Mindy was very sick when she was little and it caused her to lose some of her hearing."

Developmental Delay

Developmental disability is a term that includes a variety of disabilities that affect how a child grows and learns. While most infants and young children develop skills such as sitting and crawling at about the same age, some children develop much slower. Signs of a significant delay may become evident yet a diagnosis may not be clear. With the label of developmental delay, children are able to receive services without the concern of an unsure diagnosis or an inaccurate label. With early intervention, many at-risk children diagnosed as having a developmental delay will grow up without a disability, others will have a disability diagnosed about the time they are five or six years of age (Deiner, 1993).

People who have mental retardation are often referred to as having a developmental disability. It's important to understand that even though persons with mental retardation have a developmental delay, not all people who have a developmental delay have mental retardation. Some common developmental disabilities are: mental retardation, cerebral palsy, deafness, autism, and blindness (Meyer, et al., 1985).

Emotional and Behavioral Disorders

It is difficult to define emotional and behavioral disorders because there is no universally accepted definition. It is especially difficult at an early age because all children display emotional - behavioral problems at some time during their development. To determine if the behavior is a disorder it's necessary to look at the length, severity, and unacceptableness of it. Behavior that is disturbed involves significant changes in the child's mood and behavior and is displayed across many situations and settings. These behaviors interfere with the child's overall learning and the development of interpersonal relationships. These behaviors may also be harmful to the child or others (Deiner, 1993).

Achenbach has divided emotional - behavioral problems into two categories. Externalizing behaviors include aggressiveness, destructiveness, temper tantrums, attention-seeking behaviors (hitting and biting), hurting others, swearing, and name-calling. These behaviors involve striking out at another so there is a victim. Internalizing behaviors include withdrawal, anxiety, crying, depression, unresponsiveness, shyness, timidity, and isolation (Deiner, 1993).

Some of the behaviors listed above are common for children during certain stages of their development. When the behaviors appear during these expected times, they are considered normal behaviors. If the behaviors become excessive or persist beyond the expected age or developmental stage, the behaviors would be considered emotional - behavioral problems. (Deiner, 1993). Programming for children with emotional - behavioral problems includes a behavior management plan that can make the environment safe, secure and predictable for the child and his or her peers.

Attention Deficit Disorder With and Without Hyperactivity (ADD and ADHD)

ADHD – attention deficit with hyperactivity disorder is not a disease, it is the way the brain works which includes a short attention span, impulsivity, distractibility and **hyperactivity**. Studies have shown that individuals with ADHD may have less chemical activity and blood flow in parts of the brain which may explain these behaviors (Kajander, 1995). When children have these symptoms but do not have hyperactivity they are referred to as having **ADD** – attention deficit disorder. Children with ADD are often under diagnosed because they are not disruptive.

Children with ADHD seem to have little tolerance for frustration, often having rapid mood changes. Because of their short attention span, they appear to have random, erratic behavior and may "flit" about the environment. This combination of behaviors reduces the child's ability to engage in activities that promote learning (Peterson, 1987). An effective approach for working with these children is the use of behavior management techniques. These techniques build in structure which these children lack and help children remember what they should and should not do. The children have to deal with the consequences of their behavior when it is inappropriate and receive reinforcement for behavior that is appropriate (Batshaw & Perret, 1992).

Sometimes behavior management alone is not sufficient in helping these children and medication is used in conjunction with a behavior program which has been very effective for many children. Two good resources for information regarding the criteria for diagnosing ADHD and the use of medication are *Children with Disabilities: A Medical Primer* and *Living with ADHD: A Practical Guide to Coping with Attention Deficit Hyperactivity Disorder*.

Children may ask about inappropriate behavior or behavioral outbursts. It's important to help children understand that the child with ADHD is working hard to act appropriately, the behavior is difficult to manage and that it's the behavior we don't like, not the child.

Learning Disability

The definition used nationwide is from Public Law 94-142 (Federal Register, December 29, 1977, Part 3):

> 'Specific learning disability' means a disorder in one or more of the basic psychological processes involved in understanding or in using language, spoken or written, which may manifest itself in an imperfect ability to listen, think, speak, read, write, spell, or to do mathematical calculations. The term includes conditions such as perceptual handicaps brain injury, minimum brain dysfunction, dyslexia and developmental aphasia. The term does not include children who have learning problems which are primarily the result of visual, hearing, or motor handicaps, of mental retardation, of emotional disturbance, or of environmental, cultural, or economic disadvantage.

While there is little agreement regarding the definition of a learning disability, four criterion have been identified that are a part of all definitions: 1) there is a discrepancy between the child's tested intelligence and his or her performance in the classroom, 2) the learning disability is not due to another identified disability (e.g. mental retardation), 3) children with a learning disability have difficulty processing information in that they are not able to perceive or interpret accurately, and 4) there is dysfunction in the central nervous system (Deiner, 1993).

Many of the descriptors of a learning disability are related to reading, writing, spelling, and mathematics. Because of this, and the assessment process that is used, it is impossible to identify learning disabilities in preschool age children. However, some young children may have difficulty learning and exhibit patterns suspicious of a learning disability which may or may not be diagnosed as the child becomes older. The exact label is not important, rather an understanding of the child's problems with appropriate adaptations made so the child can experience success in learning.

Mental Retardation

The definition from the American Association of Mental Deficiency is most widely used. According to this definition, a person with mental retardation has the following : 1) significantly subaverage general intellectual functioning which is assessed by a standardized intelligence test, 2) impairment in adaptive behavior which includes functional skills for daily living which lead to personal independence and social responsibility, and 3) the age of onset occurred during the developmental years (i.e. between birth and 18 years) (Peterson, 1989).

There are three levels of retardation which generally indicate the type and intensity of services needed. **Mild** mental retardation occurs with an IQ 50-55 to 70-75. These children learn more slowly and may not be noticed during the preschool years. They tend to be immature and develop their language more slowly. Most often these individuals will be able to live independently and have a job after completing school. **Moderate** mental retardation is when the person has an IQ of 35-40 to 50-55. These children will have a significant delay in all areas of development. Their training focuses mostly on self-help and functional skills. In adulthood they usually live in supervised settings. People with **severe** mental retardation have an IQ 20-25 to 35-40 and **profound** mental retardation have an IQ below 20-25. These children are severely delayed, have few communication skills and need intensive services (Denier, 1993).

Characteristics that occur in children with mild mental retardation more often than children with normal development are: sensory and motor coordination disabilities, low tolerance for frustration, poor self-concept, short attention span, below average language ability, below average ability to generalize and conceptualize, and play interests younger than those of peers. It's unlikely that all of these characteristics would be present (Milota, et al., 1991).

Mental retardation affects a child's ability to learn, to understand and get along in the environment. Children who have mental retardation learn more slowly and may not be able to learn some of the things other children learn. Children may ask why another child is unable to do a task. Your answer might be: "Peter needs some more time at this activity before he's ready to move on to the next." OR "Peter learns, he just learns more slowly."

Down Syndrome

Down syndrome is a form of mental retardation that is present at birth with a tremendous degree of variation in the amount of retardation. These children can be visually identified by the simian crease in the palms of the hands and the "Asian" eyefolds as well as other physical anomalies. A genetic workup is done to confirm the diagnosis.

Children with Down syndrome are considered at risk as this condition is known to result in mental retardation, physical abnormalities, and delays in other areas of development such as speech and language, and motor development (Peterson, 1989). However, in the past there were low expectations and negative self-fulfilling prophecies for individuals with Down syndrome. Today with early intervention and better medical and educational services, children with Down syndrome are functioning at increasingly higher levels (Stray-Gundersen, 1986).

Multiple Disabilities

Public Law 94-142 defines multi-disabled as "those children with more than one serious disability (e.g. mental retardation and blindness, deafness and blindness), the combination of which causes such severe educational problems that they cannot be accommodated in special education programs solely for one of the impairments" (Milota, et al., 1991, p. 84). These children have very special needs and present a special challenge for educators and parents. Educational programs are designed with a team of parents and specially trained professionals who can address the variety of special needs.

Physical Disability

Physical impairments are classified according to three criteria: 1) the severity, 2) the clinical type, and 3) the parts of the body that are affected. **Mild** impairment - these children can walk (with or without aids), communicate to make their wants and needs known, and use their arms. Their problems are mostly with fine motor tasks. With adaptation, they can do what most other children can do. **Moderate** impairment - these children need help with movement and need assistance with self-help skills and communication. **Severe** impairment – these children are usually unable to move around without the aid of a wheelchair and need considerable help with self-help and communication.

Occupational therapists work with children in the development of fine motor skills which includes eating and dressing. **Physical therapists** work with children in the development of gross motor skills including mobility with the use of aids as is needed (i.e. wheelchair, leg braces).

Children will ask about the boy or girl who uses aids. They may be fearful of "catching" whatever the child has. Some might be curious how the equipment works, others may be frightened. Whenever possible, let the children examine the equipment and even try it out, always with the permission of the child who uses the equipment and with close supervision. Keeping in mind the cognitive levels of the children asking questions, help them understand the disability and why the equipment is being used. This information will help reduce or eliminate fears they may have.

Cerebral Palsy

Cerebral palsy is caused by damage to the brain before it is mature. It is a non progressive condition and involves various types of impairment in fine and gross motor development. **Anoxia** or lack of oxygen to the brain and brain injury at birth are the most frequent causes of cerebral palsy. (Deiner, 1993; Peterson, 1989).

Cerebral palsy is classified according to seven different types: 1) spastic - loss of voluntary muscle control is the most common type. Muscles are tight (hypertonic) from too much muscle tone; 2) athetosis - excessive involuntary, purposeless movements of the limbs; 3) rigid - severe spasticity; the affected limbs are rigid and extremely difficult to bend; 4) ataxia - lack of balance, uncoordinated movement and lack of a sense of position in space; 5) tremor - shakiness of the affected limbs apparent only when a specific movement occurs; and 6) atonia or hypotonia - lack of muscle tone and inability to move or maintain postural control; child is floppy (Peterson, 1989).

The following terms are used to indicate which limbs are affected: **Hemiplegia**: one side of the body is involved; **Diplegia**: legs more involved than arms; **Quadriplegia**: all four limbs are involved; **Paraplegia**: only the legs; **Monoplegia**: only one limb; **Triplegia**: three limbs are involved (Deiner, 1993).

Cerebral palsy is no longer considered to be just a motor problem rather a multidimensional disorder. Neurological, cognitive and perceptual dysfunction are the underlying and associated impairments. All areas need to be considered during intervention (Peterson, 1989).

Spina Bifida

Spina bifida is a congenital malformation of the spinal cord that is present at birth. The most common form and most serious causing lasting effects is **myelomenigocele**. The spinal cord does not close and protrudes looking like a bubble or sac on the baby's back. This is surgically closed shortly after birth. The deformity can occur anywhere along the spinal cord from the head to the lower end, however, most occur toward the lower end. The severity of the condition depends upon the location of the opening on the spine. The higher the opening, the greater the number of body parts affected. A weakness or complete paralysis of the legs, feet, bladder, and bowels, each affected in varying degrees is possible. Often there is no feeling in the buttocks and legs. When the opening is higher on the spinal cord it can affect bowel and bladder control. A high percentage of these children also develop **hydrocephalus** also known as water on the brain. This requires a shunt, inserted surgically, to drain the water. This surgery is usually done the first week after the birth. There can be some cognition problems as a result of the hydrocephalus (Deiner, 1993; Milota, et al., 1991; Peterson, 1989).

Loss of Limb

Children can be missing an arm or leg as a result of accidents, infections, or diseases such as cancer. In addition, sometimes children are born without a limb as a result of congenital malformations. Preschool children are generally not fitted for an artificial limb as physicians prefer to wait until they are older and better able to learn how to use the device (Peterson, 1989). As children get older, most are fitted with a **prosthesis** which is an artificial hand, arm, foot, or leg. With therapy, these children can learn most self-help skills and become very independent at home and school. Children will be curious and want to know how the limb was lost and how the artificial limb works. The child can be invited to share how the prosthesis works, making it a choice (in private), in case the child doesn't feel comfortable sharing.

Dwarfism or Short-Limbed

The most common type of Dwarfism is **achondroplastic dwarf**. This is caused by a genetic abnormality that affects the skeletal system (Kuklin, 1986). Dwarfism occurs when there is an abnormality of the bones causing all of the long bones to be short and stubby resulting in the child having shortened arms and legs with a disproportionately large head (Bradshaw & Perret, 1992).

Dwarfism does not limit the person's life span nor does it affect their intellectual capabilities. However, persons with dwarfism are susceptible to physiological problems relating to the skeletal and nervous system. The Little People of America is a support group for people with dwarfism (Kuklin, 1986).

Muscular Dystrophy

Muscular dystrophy is a name given to a group of diseases characterized by the chronic, progressive degeneration and weakening of voluntary muscles (e.g. those in the arms and legs). **Duchene** muscular dystrophy is the most common form which affects only male children. It is inherited and transmitted through a defective gene. The onset of this disease is usually between the ages of two and six.

There is no cure for Duchene muscular dystrophy. There isn't any medication or treatment that can slow or stop this progressive degeneration of muscle tissue. The first symptoms might be that parents notice the child becoming clumsy and falling down a lot due to muscle weakness. Tip-toe walking occurs. As the disease progresses the child may have difficulty getting up from a sitting or lying position. A waddling gait may appear. There is a continued weakening and decline in muscle strength and health. Some of the child's muscles may appear enlarged which is due to the replacement of healthy tissue with fat and fibrous tissue. Over time orthopedic devices are needed and sometimes surgery to continue mobility. Eventually a wheelchair is needed. The disease itself is painless and does not effect intellectual functioning. As the disease progresses, there is increased disability and ultimately death most often by age twenty-one (Deiner, 1993; Milota et al., 1991; Peterson, 1989).

Speech and Language

Speech problems exist when children have difficulty with the production of sounds which includes the planned shaping of sounds into specific vowel and consonant utterances (Deiner, 1993). Speech disorders generally come under three types: 1) **articulation** disorders are irregularities in the production of vowels and consonants, 2) **voice** disorders are problems with appropriate pitch, volume or voice quality, and 3) **fluency** disorders are irregularities in the flow or rhythm (Peterson, 1989).

Language problems exist when children have difficulty understanding what others say (**receptive** language) or have difficulty expressing ideas in words and sentences (**expressive** language) (Milota, et al., 1991).

Speech and language problems can exist without any other type of disability or in combination with identified disabilities. Some children have such severe speech and language disorders that they cannot learn to speak and manual communication (i.e. sign language, finger spelling) becomes the preferred method of communication. For those who are unable to sign, communication boards and microcomputers present other options.

Cleft lip – palate

Cleft lip is a narrow division in the lip and cleft palate is a narrow division in the roof of the mouth. These occur when two parts of the lip or palate fail to join properly. A cleft palate leaves a gap between the mouth and nasal cavity which may vary in size and involvement. Children with this birth defect have difficulty articulating some speech sounds. Corrective surgery is done to close the gap which will reduce or eliminate speech difficulties. Many of these children need to have therapy to correct their speech (Deiner, 1993).

References

Amenta, C.A. (1992). *Russell is extra special: A book about autism for children.* New York: Magination Press.

Bailey, D. (1992). Guidelines for authors. *Journal of Early Intervention,* 15 (1), 118-119.

Batshaw, M.L., & Perret, Y.M. (1992). *Children with disabilities: A medical primer (3rd Ed.).* Baltimore, MA: Paul H. Brookes.

Blaska, J.K. (1993). The power of language: Speak and write using "person first." In M. Nagle (Ed.), *Perspectives on disability* (pp. 25-32). Palto Alto, CA: Health Markets Research.

Deiner, P.L. (1993). *Resources for teaching children with diverse abilities.* New York, NY: Harcourt Brace Jovanovich College Publishers.

Derman-Sparks, L. (1989). *Anti-bias curriculum.* Washington, DC: NAEYC.

Eberlein, D.L. (1988). *The handbook of drugs for children with special needs.* Minneapolis, MN: Drugwise Communications.

Epidemiology Departments. (1987, January). Cleaning and Disinfection. (Available from the Minnesota Department of Health, St. Paul, MN)

Federal Register. (1977). Public Law 94-142, Education of the Handicapped Act. Washington, DC: US Department of Health, Education and Welfare.

Hadley, R.G., & Brodwin, M. B. (1988). Language about people with disabilities. *Journal of Counseling and Development*, 67, 147-149.

Hallahan, D., & Kauffman, J. (1994). *Exceptional children: Introduction to special education*. Englewood Cliffs, NJ: Prentice-Hall.

Hanft, B. (1989). How words create images. In B. E. Hanft (Ed.), *Family-centered care: An early intervention resource manual* (pp. 277-278). Rockville, MA: American Occupational Therapy Association, Inc.

Kailes, J. (1985). Watch your language, please! *Journal of Rehabilitation, 51* (1), 68-69.

Kajander, R. (1995). *Living with ADHD: A practical guide to coping with attention deficit hyperactivity disorder*. Minneapolis, MN: Park Nicollet Medical Foundation.

Kuklin, S. (1986). *Thinking big*. New York: Lothrop, Lee & Shepard Books.

Meyer, D.J., Vadasy, P.F.,& Fewell, R.R. (1985). *Living with a brother or sister with special needs*. Seattle: University of Washington Press.

Milota, C., Goldberg, M., Goldberg, P., Skaalen, J., Dahl, L., Jordan, D., Binkard, B., Edmunds, P., Leaf, R., & Steeber, B. (1991). *Count me in: Resource manual on disabilities*. Minneapolis, MN: PACER Center, Inc.

PACER. (1989, September). It's the 'person first' - Then the disability. *Pacesetter*. Mpls., MN: Parent Advocacy Coalition for Educational Rights.

Perske, R. (1988). *Circle of Friends*. Nashville, TN: The Pathenon Press.

Peterson, N.L. (1987). *Early intervention for handicapped and at risk children*. Denver, Co: Love Publishing Co.

Powers, M.D. (Ed.). (1989), *Children with Autism*. Rockville, MD: Woodbine House.

Reisner, H. (Ed.). (1988). *Children with epilepsy: A parents' guide*. Rockville, MD: Woodbine House.

Stray-Gundersen, K. (1986). *Babies with Down syndrome*. Rockville, MD: Woodbine Press.

Tyler, L. (1990). Communicating about people with disabilities: Does the language we use make a difference? *The Bulletin of the Association for Business Communication*, 53 (3), 65-67.

········

Notes

....
Notes

CHAPTER FIVE

Selecting and Reviewing Books That Incorporate Disability and Chronic Illness

The process used to select children's literature for this project that include individuals with disabilities or illness is outlined in this chapter. The review process of each book which generated the information for the annotated bibliography is also described.

Book Selection

Children's books that include individuals with a disability or chronic illness were identified through current award-winning and widely recommended book lists, publishers, book stores and catalogs of children's books. The majority of the books selected have been published since 1985. Ten were published between 1973 and 1979. Some of the earlier published books are frequently found in schools and libraries and are being routinely used with young children. Thus, it seemed appropriate to review and include some of them. However, the emphasis was on locating and reviewing more recently published books as they generally reflect the philosophy of today which include respect and responsibility, issues of inclusion, and the use of "person first" language. Sixty-six books in this collection have been published since 1990.

Efforts were made to find books at university, school and public libraries. The inter-library loan systems were also utilized. In addition, a variety of book stores were used as resources. It was not possible to locate all of the identified books in libraries or bookstores. In some cases, it was necessary to order books directly from the publisher. If your local bookstore is unable to get a particular book, you may be able to order it directly from the publisher. See Appendix B for a list of publishers of the children's books included in this project.

Review and Rating

All books were first considered using standard criteria for reviewing any children's literature specifically, characterization, setting, plot, theme, narrative and illustrations (Sawyer & Comer, 1991). In addition, each book was reviewed by Blaska using the *Images and Encounters Profile* which was developed as a checklist to review children's books for inclusion and depiction of persons with disabilities (Blaska & Lynch, 1994). The Profile contains 15 criteria that address the tone of the story, attitudes, information presented, language used, integration, and art style. For each criterion, the reviewer is to indicate YES, if the criterion was addressed positively in the story; NO, if the criterion was addressed negatively and NP if the criterion was not present in the storyline, illustrations, or language.

Images and Encounters Profile
A Checklist to Review Books for Inclusion and Depiction of Persons with Disabilities

Book Title _____

For each item below, indicate whether you believe the criteria are evidenced or not evidenced in the STORYLINE, LANGUAGE, OR ILLUSTRATIONS. Check YES if the criterion was addressed **positively**, check NO if the criterion was addressed **negatively**, and check NP if the criterion was **not present** in the storyline, illustrations, or language.

YES responses are preferred responses.
The reviewer is cautioned to be aware of the NO responses when reading and/or discussing the books as these responses may influence your use and adaptation of the book. For example, a NO response to Item 7 may result in a discussion of behaviors and feelings with the parent and/or teacher modeling respect for all persons.

YES	NO	NP	
____	____	____	1. Promotes empathy not pity
____	____	____	2. Depicts acceptance not ridicule
____	____	____	3. Emphasizes success rather, or in addition to, failure
____	____	____	4. Promotes positive images of person[s] with disabilities
____	____	____	5. Addresses abilities and disabilities
____	____	____	6. Assists children in gaining accurate understanding of the disability
____	____	____	7. Demonstrates respect for person[s] with disabilities
____	____	____	8. Promotes attitude of "one of us" not "one of them"
____	____	____	9. Depicts valued occupations for person[s] with disabilities
____	____	____	10. Uses language which stresses person first, disability second philosophy [e.g., Jody who is blind]

YES   NO   NP

____ ____ ____   11. Describes the disability or person[s] with disabilities as realistic [i.e., not subhuman or not superhuman]

____ ____ ____   12. Depicts person[s] with disabilities in integrated settings and/or activities

____ ____ ____   13. Illustrates characters in a realistic manner

____ ____ ____   14. Uses similar art styles for persons with and without disabilities

____ ____ ____   15. Illustrates accuracy in technical detail of equipment

When in doubt about using a particular book which includes a person with a disability, ask yourself, "*Would this story embarrass or humiliate a child with a disability?* If the answer is Yes, consider carefully how to best use this book.

This checklist was developed through the Images & Encounters Project, grant H-133C-10157 awarded by USOE to St. Cloud State University with a sub-contract to Moorhead State University.

With minor wording adaptations, the profile was also used to review books about chronic illness. Each annotated bibliography provides a brief summary of the story and describes strengths or concerns that became apparent after using the profile. Each book was rated based on the outcome of the review using a four-star system:

Outstanding	****
Very Good	***
Fair	**
Not Recommended	*

The *Profile* doesn't use a rating system. This system was developed after completing the review of the books and finding that the books seemed to fit into four groups. There was one group of OUTSTANDING books that received the highest ratings and in almost all cases had preferred responses (YES) to all 15 criteria on the *Profile*. Books rated Very Good generally had only 1 or 2 "NO" responses with the remaining being the preferred response. Books rated FAIR generally had 2 to 5 "NO" responses. These books can be used successfully with children but the reader should be aware of the rating of the criteria in order to determine how the book can best be used. Books with a NOT RECOMMENDED rating generally showed a lack of respect for the person with the disability or chronic illness. The *Images & Encounters Profile* indicated that when in doubt about using a particular book, ask yourself, "Would this story embarrass or humiliate a child with the disability [or illness]?" In most cases, the books rated as NOT RECOMMEND have the potential of embarrassing, humiliating or providing a negative image. The books included in this collection have all received a rating of outstanding or very good.

It's important to understand that this review is not censorship. The review process is intended to provide information about a book which may influence how you use the book (e.g. with or without an adult present). The intent is that you will be able to use books more effectively by raising your awareness of issues related to the review criteria which includes strengths as well as concerns.

Identifying Disability or Illness

Part of the review process was to identify the disability or illness that was present in the story. When more than one disability or illness was identified, the book was cross-referenced according to all that were present. The disability categories that were used are consistent with those defined in Public Law 102-119, Individuals With Disabilities Education Act (IDEA - formerly P.L. 94-142). In addition to the disability, aids that were used in the story were also identified such as Braille, wheelchair, or signing. In the stories, 16 disabilities were identified from nine disability categories:

Autism
Blind, Low Vision or Partially Sighted
Deaf or Hearing Impairment
Emotional - Behavioral Disorders
      Attention Deficit Disorder (ADD)
      Attention Deficit With Hyperactivity (ADHD)
Learning Disability
Mental Retardation
      Down Syndrome
Multiple Disabilities
Physical Disability
      Cerebral Palsy
      Spina Bifida
      Loss of Limb
      Dwarfism or Short-Limbed
      Muscular Dystrophy
Speech and Language Impairment
      Cleft lip and palate

In addition, six chronic illnesses were included in stories:
      Acquired Immune Deficiency Syndrome (AIDS)
      Allergies
      Asthma
      Cancer; Leukemia
      Diabetes
      Epilepsy or Seizure Disorder

Development of Categories

When selecting a book, the way in which the disability or illness is treated or presented in the story is significant. An analysis of the books in this selection revealed three main categories:

Category A: Books provide information about disability or illness.
Category B: Books provide stories about disability or illness.
Category C: Books provide stories with character(s) with disability or illness.

Category A. Books in this category provide information about a particular disability or chronic illness or something specifically related such as guide dogs, sign language or medication. It is not a story with the development of a plot. The intent is to gain information. This category of books is particularly useful when telling children about a certain disability or illness. These books are useful for children with and without disabilities or illnesses and can be used in home and school settings.

Category B. Books in this category contain stories about a disability or chronic illness. Information about a particular disability or illness is provided in a story format with character development and a plot. The person with the disability or illness is integral to the storyline. The intent is to learn about the disability or illness or related issues (i.e. attitudes, feelings) within a story format. These stories provide an entertaining or interesting way to learn about a disability or illness. This type of book is useful for children with and without disabilities or illnesses and can be used in home and school environments.

Category C. In this category, within the story one or more of the characters have a disability or illness. The character may be integral or peripheral to the storyline. The story is not about a disability or illness rather the story has a character who happens to have a disability or illness. The story does not necessarily provide specific information about a disability or illness. However, the reader may incidentally gain some information and insight. The intent is to read the story for enjoyment with the inclusion of a character with a disability or illness. For children without disabilities or illnesses, these stories expose them to all kinds of people like those who exist in society and opens the door for questions and discussion. Children are able to see what individuals with disabilities and chronic illnesses can do and how they are like themselves yet different. This is a very natural way for children to learn about people with disabilities and illnesses who are integrated into our society.

For children with disabilities or chronic illness, stories such as these allow them to see themselves as part of the mainstream society. This can provide a boost to their self-esteem. This type of literature is important for all children but is especially important in inclusive settings so all children can see themselves represented in the literature that is being used. These stories can be used in both home and school settings.

It's unfortunate that there seems to be a limited number of books available for

Category C. Only 20% of the books reviewed for this project (24 books) fit into this category. This limited number indicates a need for more stories that integrate characters with a disability or illness into the story, either integral or peripheral to the storyline.

Theme Analysis

A curriculum theme is a general idea or concept to which a variety of materials relate (Herr & Libby, 1994). Many early childhood professionals use a theme approach as they work with young children. All of the activities for the day or several days reflect the chosen theme including the selection of books.

A review of the literature was conducted to identify the most commonly used themes. In many cases, themes were similar just given different titles (e.g. Holidays Around the World vs. each holiday identified separately). In all, 71 major themes were identified. In order to determine into which of the 71 themes each book could be effectively incorporated, a theme analysis was conducted. Overall, books were identified that could be used in 50 of the themes. Many times it was determined that a book could be appropriately incorporated into more than one theme. In those cases, the books were listed under multiple themes or units. The 50 themes include the following:

Apples
Beach Party or Seashore
Body Awareness
Brothers & Sisters
Buildings
Children and Families Around the World
Circus, Circus Animals, Clowns
City
Colors in My World
Community Workers
Day and Night
Dentist, Doctors, Nurses and Hospitals
Families
Families at Work
Farm and Farm Animals
Feelings
Fish, Fishing
Friends and School
Friendship
Giving and Sharing
Grandmothers and Grandfathers
Holidays Around the World
Hats
Health
Homes and Neighborhoods
Naptime and Bedtime
Numbers in My Everyday World

Oceans, Lakes and Rivers
Peace Education
Pet Animals
Planting or Gardening
Picnics
Safety
Shapes, Sizes and Weights
Sight (seeing)
Smell
Sound (hearing)
Sports
Spring
Summer
Taste
Tools and Machines to Use in My World
Touch
Transportation
We Are Alike, We Are Different
Wheels
Winter
Zoo Animals

References

Beckman, C., Simmons, R., & Thomas, N. (1982). *Channels to children: Early childhood activity guide for holidays and seasons.* Colorado Springs, CO: Channels Top Children.

Blaska, J.K., & Lynch, E.C. (1994). Inclusion and depiction of individuals with disabilities in award-winning and highly recommended children's books. Submitted for publication.

Brokering, L. (1989). *Resources for dramatic play.* Belmont, CA: Fearon Teacher Aids.

Carroll, J. (1983). *Lollipop learning series.* Carthage, IL: Good Apple, Inc.

Chenfeld, M.B. (1983). *Creative activities for young children.* New York: Harcourt Brace Jovanovich, Inc.

Coletta, A.J., & Coletta, K. (1986). *Year 'round activities for three-year-old children.* West Nyack, NY: Center for Applied Research in Education, Inc.

Drew, R. (1990). *Theme series – Bears: Integrated activities for whole language and thematic teaching.* Cypress, CA: Creative Teaching Press.

Federal Law. (1991). Public Law 102-119, Individuals with Disabilities Education Act (IDEA). Washington, DC: US Dept. of Health, Education, & Welfare.

Hamilton, D.S., & Flemming, B.M. (1990). *Resources for creative teaching in early childhood education, (2nd Ed.).* New York: Harcourt Brace Jovanovich Publishers.

Herr, J., & Libby, Y. (1990). *Creative resources for the early childhood classroom.* Delmar Publishers, Inc.

Herr, J. & Libby, Y. (1994). *Early Childhood Writing Centers.* New York: Harcourt Brace College Publishers.

Indenbaum, V., & Shapiro, M. (1985). *The everything book.* Livonia, MI: Partner Press.

Raines, S.C., & Canady, R.J. (1989). *Story s-t-r-e-t-c-h-e-r-s: Activities to expand children's favorite books.* Mt. Rainer, MA: Gryphon House, Inc.

Sawyer, W., & Comer, D.E. (1991). *Growing up with literature.* Albany, NY: Delmar Publishers, Inc.

Toboni, V. (1991). *Theme series – Farm animals: Integrated activities for whole language and thematic teaching.* Cypress, CA: Creative Teaching Press, Inc.

Walters, C., & Tollen, D. (1991). *Sing a song all year long.* Minneapolis, MN: T.S. Dennison & Company, Inc.

Warren, J., & Walker, C.L. (1989). *Theme-A-Saurus: The great big book of mini teaching themes.* Everett, WA: Warren Publishing House, Inc.

• • • • • • • • • • • •
CHAPTER SIX

Annotated Bibliography: Children's Books Depicting Persons with Disabilities or Chronic Illness

Introduction

An annotated bibliographic entry is provided for each book in this selection. Each entry contains the following information: author, title, illustrator, publisher, year of publication, ISBN number, number of pages, fiction or nonfiction, grade level, disability, rating, category, annotation and theme(s).

Author, Title, Illustrator. The books are listed in alphabetical order by author. Sometimes parents or professionals may be more familiar with a book according to its title. To assist in this type of search, the books have also been alphabetized by title. See Appendix C for this listing. Following the author' name is the book's title and illustrator. The majority of the books are picture books with the illustrations an integral part of the story. Thus, the illustrators and photographers are identified by name.

Publisher, Year Of Publication, ISBN. Next is the publisher and the year of publication. The majority of these books having been published since 1980, and are still in print. Most of them can be located through your library, its loan system or your local book store. However, in the event you have difficulty finding a particular book, you can contact the publisher directly. See Appendix B for a list of publishers of children's books. The ISBN number which is the book's identification number is included for each book. If you choose to purchase any of the books, it makes it easier when you have this number.

Pages, Fiction or Nonfiction, Grade Level. The number of pages is identified, whether the book is fiction or nonfiction, and the grade level for which the book is recommended. This information was obtained from the publisher or published book lists and will be helpful when selecting books appropriate for the age and developmental level of the children who will be using the books.

Please keep in mind that some children's books may be used appropriately with children older or younger than are recommended. For example, books that have lots of words may be indicated for older children but can be used for younger ones as well if you tell the story while using the illustrations. Books may be used for children older than indicated when a book gives a particular message and it is used to promote discussion. In addition, children's books can be used very successfully in parent groups to introduce topics or ideas that will then be discussed. Many children's books contain wonderful messages which allows them to be used successfully in a number of ways.

Disability Or Illness. The disability area or chronic illness is then listed. In the event that more than one disability or illness is present in the story, all are identified. Any aids that are used in the story or illustrations are also listed (i.e. wheelchair, cane). For physical disabilities, the type of disability is listed if it's available and for chronic illnesses, the type of illness is identified.

Book Rating. Each book was given one of four ratings based on the results of the review using the *Images and Encounters Profile*. In the annotations, strengths are mentioned and concerns described when they are present.

Ratings

Outstanding	****
Very Good	***
Fair	**
Not Recommended	*

Book Categories. The last part of the reference is the category of the book which is determined by the author's treatment of the disability or illness or how it is incorporated into the story. The books fit into one of three categories:

Category A: Books provide information about disability or chronic illness.
Category B: Books provide stories about a disability or chronic illness.
Category C: Stories with character(s) with disability or chronic illness.

Annotation. The annotation briefly highlights the storyline. Strengths and concerns are then indicated based on the criteria that were used in the review process.

Theme Or Unit. Each entry ends with the theme(s) or unit(s) into which the book can be appropriately incorporated based on the theme analysis. When a book is appropriate to use with more than one theme, multiple themes are listed.

Annotated Bibliography: Books Depicting Persons With Disability or Illness

Ratings

Outstanding	****
Very Good	***
Fair	**
Not recommended	*

Categories

A – Information About Disability or Illness
B – Story About Disability or Illness
C – Story with Character[s] with Disability or Illness

Alden, Joan. *A Boy's Best Friend,* **illus. by Catherine Hopkins. Alyson Publications, Inc., 1992. ISBN 1-55583-203-2 [28 p]. Fiction, Gr. PS-2. Illness: Asthma. (****) (Cat C).**
Willy wants a dog for his birthday but every year he is told that he can't have one because of his asthma. This year his special gift is LeDogg, a wooly stuffed dog with Willy's name on his collar. Willy takes LeDogg everywhere including school where he encounters teasing from bullies. Some magic happens that enables Willy to get his LeDogg out of a tree. All children would enjoy this story but it would be really special for children like Willy who aren't able to have pets.
Themes or Units: **Families; Health; Pet Animals.**

Alexander, Sally Hobart. *Mom Can't See Me,* **photographs by George Ancona. Macmillan Publishing Co., 1990. ISBN 0-02-700401-5 [45 p]. Nonfiction, Gr. K-3. Disability: Blindness. (****) (Cat A)**
A young girl tells what it is like to have a mother who is blind. Leslie explains that her mother is a writer and reads using braille. Humorous events are also described such as the time her mother hugged a man at the airport who sounded like her brother! This is a very positive story as it points out what this mother can do as well as the adaptations she makes because of her blindness. The author does not use "person first" language (i.e. "handicapped person" and "blind parent"). This is a very realistic and heartwarming story.
Themes or Units: **Families; Families at Work (writer); Sight (seeing); Touch; We Are Alike, We Are Different.**

Alexander, Sally Hobart. *Mom's Best Friend,* **photographs by George Ancona. Macmillan Publishing Co., 1992. ISBN 0-02-700393-0 [45 p]. Nonfiction, Gr. K-3. Disability: Blindness. (****) (Cat A)**
This is a story about Sally and her experiences as she receives training to have a new guide dog. Black and white photographs allow the reader to see the training episodes to prepare the guide dog who will eventually be able to work with its new master. In the end, the entire family gains a pet. This is a very informative and sensitive story that will help children understand blindness and the use of guide dogs. It promotes a positive image as Sally is shown being independent and capable.
Themes or Units: **Pet Animals; Sight (seeing).**

Allen, Anne. *Sports for the Handicapped.* **Walker Publishing Co., 1981. ISBN 0-8027-6436-3 [78 p]. Nonfiction, Gr. 1-3. Disability: Physical, Blindness, Mental Retardation, Deafness. (***) (Cat A)**

The introduction provides a short history of people with disabilities participating in sports. Each chapter describes one of six sports in which persons with disabilities participate: skiing, wheelchair basketball, swimming, track and field, football, and horseback riding. Most participants have physical disabilities, however, blindness, mental retardation, and deafness are also represented. The emphasis is on what individuals with disabilities can do and could provide hope to children with disabilities that they, too, may one day participate. The story does not use "person first" language.

Themes or Units: **Sports; Wheels.**

Althea. *I Have Diabetes,* **illus. by Angela Owen. Dinosaur Publications, 1991. ISBN 0-851-22809-7 [30 p]. Nonfiction, K-3. Chronic Illness: Diabetes. (****) (Cat A)**

This is a story about a young girl who has diabetes. The reader learns about diabetes and the human body's need for insulin. The young girl is very independent giving herself her own shots, testing her blood and staying overnight with friends. An excellent book for helping children learn about diabetes. The story promotes a positive image and stresses the attitude of "one of us." This author has a second book *I Have Epilepsy* which follows this same format.

Themes or Units: **Health.**

Amadeo, Diane M. *There's A Little Bit Of Me In Jamey,* **illus. by Judith Friedman. Albert Whitman & Co., 1989. ISBN 0-8-75-7854-1 [32 p]. Nonfiction, Gr. 1-4. Chronic Illness: Cancer. (****) (Cat B)**

Brian wakes up and finds that his little brother who has leukemia had become very ill during the night and was taken to the hospital. Jamey is very sick and needs a bone morrow transplant. The only possible donor is Brian, who wants to donate but is scared. His parents assure him he'll be all right. When Brian wakes up his hip hurts a little but he doesn't mind because now a little bit of him is in Jamey and maybe now his brother can come home, to stay. This is a very moving story, sensitively written. The warm pencil sketchings add to the beauty of the story.

Themes or Units: **Brothers and Sisters; Dentists, Doctors, Nurses & Hospitals; Feelings; Giving and Sharing; Grandmothers and Grandfathers; Health.**

Amenta, Charles A. *Russell is Extra Special: A Book About Autism for Children*, photos by author. Magination Press, 1992. ISBN 0-945354-44-4 [27 p]. Nonfiction, Gr. PS-2. Disability: Autism. (****) (Cat A)
Russell who has autism lives with his two brothers, his mom and dad. The story describes what it is like to have autism by talking about Russell's behaviors, what he likes and dislikes, and how he plays and communicates. This is an excellent book for children and parents to learn about autism. While it discusses Russell's behaviors and his many challenges, it also points out what he can do and clearly shows Russell as an important member of his family. Black and white photographs add to the story. The author does not use "person first" language.
Themes or Units: **Families; We Are Alike, We Are Different.**

Ancona, George and Ancona, Mary Beth. *Handtalk Zoo*, photographs by Maureen Galvani. Macmillan, 1989. ISBN 0-02-700801-0 [28 p]. Nonfiction, Gr. PS-1. Disability: Deafness. (****) (Cat B)
This story shows Mary Beth and a group of children as they visit the zoo. The children sign and finger spell the names of the animals and places that they visit. Vibrant colored photographs capture the fun the children are having. The story demonstrates how all children can enjoy using sign language or finger spelling to express themselves. This book is a companion to *Handtalk* and *Handtalk Birthday* by Remy Charlip.
Themes or Units: **Sight (seeing); Zoo animals.**

Arnold, Caroline. *A Guide Dog Puppy Grows Up*, photographs by Richard Hewett. Harcourt Brace Jovanovich, 1991. ISBN 0-15-232657-X [48 p]. Nonfiction, Gr. 1-3. Disability: Blindness. (****) (Cat B)
This book tells the story of how a guide dog is selected, socialized and trained. Honey, a golden retriever puppy lives with a 4-H family for 15 months to be socialized and then undergoes two years of training at the guide dog school. The final portion of the training takes place with the dog's future partner who is bind. During the graduation ceremony, the family who socialized the puppy, passes the leash to the dog's new owner. This book provides interesting, factual information about training guide dogs that children would enjoy. "Person first" language is not used.
Themes or Units: **Giving and Sharing; Pet Animals; Sight (seeing); We Are Alike, We Are Different.**

Barrett, Mary Brigid. *Sing To The Stars*, illlus. by Sandra Speidel. Little, Brown & Co., 1994. ISBN 0-316-08224-4 [30 p]. Fiction, Gr. PS-3. Disability: Blindness. (****)(Cat C)
Young Ephram is taking violin lessons. On his way home, he sees Mr. Washington who lives in his building out walking with his guide dog. Later he discovers that Mr. Washington is a famous pianist but hasn't touched a piano since becoming blind. Ephram convinces Mr. Washington to play music with him at the neighborhood get-together. This is a heartwarming story with African-American characters. Brilliant pastel illustrations helps set the mood and promote a positive image.
Themes or Units: **Friendship; We Are Alike, We Are Different.**

Bergman, Thomas. *Going Places: Children Living with Cerebral Palsy,* **photographs by author. Gareth Stevens Children's Books, 1991. ISBN 0-8368-0199-7 [41 p]. Nonfiction, Gr. PS-3. Disability: Cerebral Palsy (wheelchair) and Deafness (signing). (****) (Cat A)**

Mathias is a six-year-old boy with cerebral palsy. Mathias has additional challenges as he is also deaf and learning sign language. The story points out the importance of technology as Mathias practices on a computer and becomes more independent as he moves around in his new electric wheelchair. An excellent book for helping children gain an accurate understanding of cerebral palsy. Black and white photographs give the reader a clear understanding of daily events in Mathias's life. The book has a short section containing answers to questions most often asked about cerebral palsy.

Themes or Units: **Sounds (hearing); We Are Alike, We Are Different.**

Bergman, Thomas. *We Laugh, We Love, We Cry: Children Living with Mental Retardation,* **photographs by author. Gareth Stevens Inc., 1989. ISBN 1-55532-914-4 [45 p]. Nonfiction, Gr. K-3. Disability: Mental Retardation. (****) (Cat A)**

This book is about 5-year-old Asa and her sister, six-year-old Anna. Both have mental retardation with some physical problems. Neither can speak but are learning to communicate by using sign language. Photographs at school, play and home depict daily events but focus mostly on the girls' therapy. It's important for children to understand that many persons with mental retardation are able to speak. Bergman is Sweden's best-known children's photographer and has captured the feelings of these little girls, their parents and the professionals who work with them.

Themes or Units: **We Are Alike, We Are Different.**

Booth, Barbara. *Mandy,* **illus. by Jim Lamarche. Lothrop, Lee & Shepard Bks., 1991. ISBN 0-688-10338-3 [31 p]. Fiction, Gr. PS-2. Disability: Deafness. (****) (Cat C)**

Even though Mandy is deaf, she and her grandmother do many things together including a walk in the woods. Grandmother loses a small pin that is very special to her. Mandy sees grandma's tears and realizes how sad she feels. Mandy goes out to find the pin. She returns to a worried Grandma who becomes so grateful that Mandy found her pin. This story shows a wonderful relationship between grandmother and granddaughter. It promotes a positive image by showing all that Mandy does with her grandmother and the fun they have together.

Themes or Units: **Day & Night; Grandmothers & Grandfathers; Sound (hearing).**

Brown, Tricia. *Someone Special, Just Like You,* **photographs by Fran Ortiz. Henry Holt & Company, 1984. ISBN 0-8050-0481-5 [55 p]. Nonfiction, Gr. PS-2. Disabilities: Hearing and Vision, Physical, Down Syndrome. (****) (Cat A)**

Black and white photographs of children in preschool settings introduce what it is like to have a visual or hearing impairment, a physical disability or mental retardation. The message is that children with disabilities are children first who enjoy doing usual things like eating ice cream, singing, dancing, going down a slide, blowing bubbles, etc. The story emphasizes what children can do even though they have different capabilities and may experience life a bit differently. The photographs include children from diverse cultures.

Themes or Units: **Friends & School; Friendship; Safety; Sight (seeing); Sounds (hearing); Touch; We Are Alike, We Are Different.**

Bunnett, Rochelle. *Friends in The Park,* **photographs by Carl Sahlhoff. Checkerboard Press, 1992. ISBN 1-56288-347 [33 p]. Nonfiction, Gr. PS-1. Disability: Physical, Down Syndrome. (****) (Cat B)**

This book illustrates a typical day at the neighborhood park with children from diverse cultures and of varying abilities. In all, twenty children are photographed as they participate in activities such as: blowing bubbles, going down the slide, crawling through a tunnel, and having juice. Children with physical disabilities and others with Down syndrome are integrated with children without disabilities in a very natural setting. The photographs capture activities which illustrate what the children can do and promote the feeling of "one of us."

Themes or Units: **Friendship; Homes and Neighborhoods (park); Summer; We Are Alike, We Are Different.**

Bunting, Eve. *The Sunshine Home,* **illus. by Diane De Grout. Clarion Books, 1994. ISBN 0-395-63309-5 [32 p]. Nonfiction, Gr. K-3. Disability: Physical (wheelchairs & walker). (****) (Cat B)**

Tim and his parents visit Grams at the nursing home. When they arrive, she looks great and seems happy. But when they get outside, Tim's mother starts to cry. Tim runs back in to give Gram his picture and finds Gram crying too. Through Tim's efforts, they all share and are honest about their feelings. This story is very heartwarming and realistic. Through the story children can become aware of the challenges of caring for the elderly. The illustrations capture the emotions experienced by the characters.

Themes or Units: **Dentist, Doctors, Nurses & Hospitals; Families; Feelings; Grandmother & Grandfather; Health.**

Bunting, Eve. *The Wall,* **illus. by Ronald Hilmer. Clarion Books, 1990. ISBN 0-395-51588-2 [32 p]. Fiction, Gr. PS-3. Disability: Physical. (****) (Cat C)**

A father and son visit the Vietnam Memorial Wall in Washington D.C. to find the name of the boy's grandfather who was killed in the war. While at the wall they see other people including a veteran with a physical disability. The water-color illustrations support the simple text and capture the many feelings associated with this experience. The story provides a wonderful opportunity to discuss what it might be like to have a disability promoting empathy and disability awareness. The character with the disability is in illustration only.
Themes or Units: **Families; Feelings; Peace Education; We Are Alike, We Are Different.**

Cairo, Shelley. *Our Brother Has Down's Syndrome,* **photographs by Irene McNeil. Annick Press LTD., 1985. ISBN 0-920303-31-5 [21 p]. Nonfiction, Gr. K-3. Disability: Down Syndrome. (****) (Cat A)**

Jai is a toddler who has Down syndrome. His two older sisters describe what it means to have Down syndrome and lovingly tell about their brother, pointing out all of the things that Jai likes such as eating ice-cream, wading in the water and getting into his sister's things. The message is that Jai may be a little different but we all have some differences. The story is sensitively written and promotes a positive attitude about a child with Down syndrome. The story does not utilize "person first" language and incorrectly refers to Down syndrome as Down's syndrome.
Themes or Units: **Brothers & Sisters; Families; We Are Alike, We Are Different.**

Calmenson, Stephanie. *Rosie: A Visiting Dog's Story,* **photographs by Justin Sutcliffe. Clarion, 1994. ISBN 0-316-08224-4 [47 p]. Nonfiction, Gr. PS-3. Illness and Disability. (***) (Cat A)**

Rosie is a working dog or also called a Therapy Dog. This is a story about how she is trained and what Rosie does when she is working. In this story, Rosie visits young and old people with disabilities or illnesses and helps cheer them up. Vivid colored photographs capture Rosie's personality and the many emotions expressed by the people she visits. This story clearly shows that people with disabilities and illness have feelings just like anybody else.
Themes or Units: **Feelings; Giving and Sharing; Pet Animals.**

Carlson, Nancy. *Arnie and the New Kid,* **illus. by author. Viking Penguin, 1990. ISBN 0-14-050945-3 [28 p]. Fiction, Gr. PS-3. Disability: Physical (wheelchair). (****)(Cat B)**

Philip is a new boy at school who uses a wheelchair. Sometimes he needs help, but many times he does not. An anthropomorphic approach is used in this story with Philip and the other children depicted as animals. Arnie teases Philip until one day Arnie falls and breaks his leg, twists a wrist, and sprains his tail. With these injuries, Arnie is not as capable as he had once been. After this accident, the boys become friends and do everything together. The story promotes friendships between children with and without disabilities.
Themes or Units: **Feelings; Friends & School; Friendship; Giving & Sharing; We Are Alike, We Are Different.**

Caseley, Judith. *Apple Pie and Onions,* **illus. by author. Greenwillow Books, 1987. ISBN 0-688-06763-8 [27 p]. Fiction, Gr. K-3. Disability: Physical (wheelchair). (****) (Cat C)**

Rebecca enjoys the stories that her Grandma tells. During one of her visits, they go for a walk. Grandma is excited to see Hattie, a friend who is in a wheelchair. She talks loudly to her in Yiddish and Rebecca is embarrassed. After Grandma tells a story about a time when she was embarrassed, Rebecca decides to have tea with Grandma and together they make an apple pie. This is a sensitive story about the relationship between a granddaughter and her grandmother. The story promotes a positive image of a person with a disability as Grandma treats Hattie special and is excited to see her.

Themes or Units: **Apples, Grandmothers and Grandfathers, Feelings (embarrassment).**

Caseley, Judith. *Harry and Willy and Carrothead,* **illus. by author. Greenwillow Books, 1991. ISBN 0-688-09492-9 [20 p]. Fiction, Gr. K-3. Disability: Physical (prosthesis for left hand). (****) (Cat B)**

When Harry was born, his left arm ended at the elbow. At school, the children ask questions about his prothesis. They soon learn that Harry can play and eat like a "regular kid." Eventually, Harry, Willy and Carrothead become best friends. This story illustrates that children are teased for many reasons (i.e. disability, differences such as hair color). The story takes place in an integrated program and promotes a positive image of someone with a physical disability by illustrating the many things Harry is able to do. The illustrations are colorful and include children from diverse cultures.

Themes or Units: **Feelings; Friendship and School; Friendship; We Are Alike, We Are Different.**

Chaplin, Susan Gibbons. *I Can Sign My ABCs,* **illus. Laura McCaul. Kendall Green Publisher, 1986. ISBN 0-930323-19-X [52 p]. Nonfiction, PS-2. Disability: Deafness, Hearing Loss. (****) (Cat A)**

This book is an introduction to the alphabet in sign language. On each set of two pages, the left page shows a hand demonstrating the manual handshape for a letter of the alphabet while the right page has a picture of a child demonstrating the sign for a common object that begins with that same letter. Large, brightly colored illustrations help the reader learn the signs. This would be a good book for children just learning to sign. The colorful illustrations add to its appeal.

Themes or Units: **Sight (seeing).**

Charlip, Remy. *Handtalk Birthday,* **photographs by George Ancona. MacMillan, 1987. ISBN 0-02-718080-8 [44 p]. Nonfiction, Gr. K-3. Disability: Deafness. (****) (Cat B)**

A group of Mary Beth's friends surprise her with gifts and a party for her birthday. Mary Beth dresses outrageously which adds humor to the story. The colorful photographs show the reader how to sign and fingerspell. This book is a companion to Handtalk and Handtalk Zoo by the same author and photographer.

Themes or Units: **Giving and Sharing; Sounds (hearing); We Are Alike, We Are Different.**

Coerr, Eleanor. *Sadako,* **illus. by Ed Young. G.P. Putnam's Sons, 1993. ISBN 0-399-21771-1 [45 p]. Nonfiction, Gr. 2-6. Illness: Leukemia. (****) (Cat B)**

Sadako is a twelve year old Japanese girl who develops leukemia, the "atom bomb disease," ten years after the bomb was dropped on Hiroshima. The story tells of Sadako's struggles to survive including the legend of a sick person folding 1,000 paper cranes so the gods will grant that person a wish to be well again. Because of the historic significance of this story, children will want to read Sadako, which is a very moving story.

Themes and Units: **Health; Holidays Around the World; Peace Education.**

Cohen, Miriam. *It's George,* **illus. by Lillian Hoban. Greenwillow Books, 1988. ISBN 0-688-06812-X [29 p]. Fiction, Gr. PS-3. Disability: Mental Retardation or Learning Disability. (***) (Cat B)**

George is in first grade. Because reading and writing are difficult for him, some of the children call him "dumb." Each day on his way to school George stops at his friend's house, 79 year old Mr. Emmons. One morning Mr. Emmons has fallen out of his chair so George calls 911 and help comes. Now all his classmates like George. This story perpetuates the hero theme for persons with differences; George should be accepted for who he is without needing to become superhuman. George's schooling takes place in an integrated setting with children from diverse cultures.

Themes or Units: **Friendship; Safety.**

Cohen, Miriam. *See You Tomorrow, Charles,* **illus. by Lillian Hoban. Dell Publishing, 1983. ISBN 0-440-40162-3 [28 p]. Fiction, Gr. PS-2. Disability: Blindness. (***) (Cat B)**

Charles is blind and in first grade. The story describes many activities in which Charles participates and the feelings and perceptions of his classmates. Charles is very capable and guides his friends out of a dark basement in which the children had gone as they played a pretend game. The story portrays Charles as a "hero". The story does takes place in an integrated setting and stresses what Charles can do as well as what he cannot do. The story incorporates diversity of ability as well as cultural diversity.

Themes or Units: **Friends & School; Sight (seeing); We Are Alike, We Are Different.**

Condra, Estelle. *See The Ocean,* **illus. by Linda Crockett-Blassingame. Ideals Children's Books, 1994. ISBN 1-57102-005-5 [29 p]. Fiction, Gr. K-3. Disability: Blindness. (****) (Cat C)**

Each year, Nellie, her parents and two older brothers travel across the mountains to their beach house on the ocean. The children always try to be first to see the ocean from the top of the mountains. This year it's cloudy and misty and no one can see but Nellie. She describes the ocean but her brothers feel it's unfair because after all, she can't see. Her mom tells the boys, "Though your sister's eyes are blind, she can see with her mind." A sensitive story about this family's relationship. The illustrations are exquisite incandescent oil paintings.

Themes or Units: **Families; Oceans, Lakes & Rivers; Sight; Sounds (hearing); Summer; We Are Alike, We Are Different.**

Cowen-Fletcher, Jane. *Mama Zooms*, **illus. by author. Scholastic, Inc., 1993. ISBN 0-590-45774-8 [29 p]. Fiction, Gr. PS-2. Disability: Physical (wheelchair). (****) (Cat C)**
This is a story about a little boy and his mom who zooms him everywhere in her zooming machine which in reality is her wheelchair. As they zoom around, the little boy imagines he's on a train, driving a race car, riding a racehorse, etc. The mom zooms him around until it's bedtime. This is a very positive story showing the mom zooming everywhere in her wheelchair, rarely needing help. She is perceived as being able to do many things which negates the old stereotype of being "confined" to a wheelchair.
Themes or Units: **Family; Transportation; We Are Alike, We Are Different; Wheels.**

Damrell, Liz. *With The Wind*, **pictures by Stephen Marchesi. Orchard Books, 1991. ISBN 0-531-05882-4 [25 p]. Fiction, Gr. PS-2. Disability: Physical (leg braces & wheelchair). (****) (Cat C)**
A young boy goes horseback riding. As he rides he feels the strength of the horse beneath him. He feels freedom, joy and power. When he returns from his ride, his parents are waiting and his father helps him off the horse and into his wheelchair. The text of this story is a poem that reflects the sense of freedom the boy imagines as he rides. The boy's disability undoubtedly influences his feelings of freedom as he rides. The mood is set with the soft colors used in the illustrations.
Themes or Units: **Farm and Farm Animals; Feelings; Pet Animals; Transportation; We Are Alike, We Are Different.**

Delton, Judy. *I'll Never Love Anything Ever Again*, **illus. by Rodney Pate. Albert Whitman & Co., 1985. ISBN 0-8075-3521-4 [32 p]. Fiction, Gr. PS-3. Illness: Allergies. (****) (Cat B)**
This is a touching story about a young boy who must give up his dog, Tinsel, because he has become allergic to dogs. He is terribly upset but finally begins to think about how much fun Tinsel would have on a farm and that it would be fun to visit in the summer. With great sadness and tears, the young boy must say, "Good-bye" to his dog and thinks that he'll never love anything again. The blue and white illustrations help set the mood. All children would benefit from this sensitively written story. It would be a good choice for any child who has to give up his or her pet for whatever reason.
Themes or Units: **Feelings; Health; Pet Animals.**

Dwight, Laura. *We Can Do It!*, **Checkerboard Press, 1992.**
ISBN 1-56288-301-1 [30 p]. Nonfiction, Gr. PS-2. Disabilities: Spina Bifida,
Down Syndrome, Cerebral Palsy, Blindness. (****) (Cat A)
This is a book about five culturally diverse children with special needs and
what they can do. The children are introduced, their ages and disabilities identified, and then colorful photographs show activities that each child likes to
do. For example, Gina who has spina bifida likes to wheel her chair down to
the beach and play in the water. This isn't a story about disabilities rather an
explanation of what each child can realistically do. It is a very positive book
and would help children have a better understanding of what children with
disabilities can do.
Themes or Units: **Friends and School; We Are Alike, We Are Different.**

Dwyer, Kathleen M. *What Do You Mean I Have a Learning Disability?*,
photographs by Barbara Beirne. Walker and Company, 1991.
ISBN 0-8027-8103-9 [35 p]. Nonfiction, Gr. 1-5. Disability: Learning Dis-
ability. (***) (Cat A)
Jimmy has lots of trouble finding and remembering things. In school, he has a
hard time with some of the work. He thinks he is stupid. After an evaluation by
Dr. Stone, Jimmy and his parents discover that he has a learning disability. At
school he gets help from a tutor. With hard work, his school work improves
and he starts to feel better about himself. A good story to learn what it feels
like to have a learning disability.
Themes or Units: **Feelings; We Are Alike, We Are Different.**

Edwards, Michelle. *alef-bet – A Hebrew Alphabet Book*, **illus. by author.**
Lothrop, Lee & Shepard Books, 1992. ISBN 0-688-09724-3 [26 p]. Nonfic-
tion, Gr. K-2. Disability: Physical (wheelchair). (****) (Cat C)
This is a delightful book about the Hebrew alphabet. It is illustrated with
bright, colorful pictures. One family is represented throughout and one of
their children uses a wheelchair. Each time the child appears, he is depicted as
an active, capable member of the family. Using this book would be a fun way
to learn about the alphabet in another language.
Themes or Units: **Children & Families Around the World; Families.**

Emmert, Michelle. *I'm The Big Sister Now*, **illus. Gail Owens. Albert**
Whitman & Co., 1989. ISBN 0-8075-3458-7 [25 p]. Nonfiction, Gr. K-3.
Disability: Cerebral Palsy, Severe Brain Damage (multiple disabilities).
(****) (Cat A)
This story is about Amy who has multiple disabilities and is told by her sister.
While Amy is unable to do many things, the story emphasizes that she is a
person with feelings and describes how she is included by her family. As the
sister grows older and can help Amy, she feels like she has become the big sis-
ter. This story is very sensitively written with soft colored illustrations. The
story promotes a positive image by showing how Amy is loved by her family.
Children would clearly gain an understanding of what it is like to have multiple disabilities with the information presented.
Themes or Units: **Brothers and Sisters; Families; We Are Alike, We Are Dif-**
ferent.

Gaes, Jason. *My Book For Kids With Cansur*, illus. by Tim & Adam Gaes. Melius & Peterson, 1988. ISBN 0-937603-04-X [32 p]. Nonfiction, Gr. PS-4. **Chronic Illness: Cancer. (****) (Cat A)**

This story was written by eight-year-old Jason. He wants to tell children what it's like to have cancer and that everyone who gets cancer does not die. The text is in Jason's own handwriting (printing) with words spelled the way he wrote them. He explains about his own cancer, the tests, and all of the procedures he has experienced. He also tells all the good things about having cancer as well as the not so good. His two brothers illustrated the book with drawings that help tell the story. This book would be helpful when talking to young children about cancer. It is factual yet very positive.

Themes or Units: **Dentists, Doctors, Nurses & Hospitals; Health.**

Gehret, Jeanne. *Eagle Eyes*, illus. by Susan Covert. Verbal Images Press, 1991. ISBN 0-9625136-4-4 [27 p]. Fiction, Gr. 1-5. **Disability/Illness: Attention Deficit Disorder. (****) (Cat B)**

On a nature walk, Ben's loudness and carelessness frightens all of the birds away. At school he has trouble paying attention and remembering his school work. Ben is diagnosed and treated for Attention Deficit Disorder. When he and his family return to the park, Ben is the one who is able to help his dad out in an emergency. A very realistic yet positive story about a family living with a son who has ADD.

Themes or Units: **Brothers and Sisters; Families; Feelings; Health; We Are Alike, We Are Different.**

Girard, Linda Walvoord. *Alex, the Kid With AIDS*, illus. by Blanche Sims. Albert Whitman & Co., 1991. ISBN 0-8075-0247-2 [29 p]. Fiction, Gr. 1-4. **Chronic Illness: AIDS. (***) (Cat B)**

The school nurse talks to the first grade class about a new classmate, Alex, who has AIDS. The children learn about the disease and that they cannot catch AIDS just by being near Alex. The story shows how funny Alex is and the fun and "trouble" he gets into. Soon, Alex becomes one of Brian's best friends. This story points out that even though Alex has AIDS, he is a typical child. This would be a good story to help children learn about AIDS.

Themes or Units: **Friends and School; Health.**

Golden, Barbara Diamond. *Cakes and Miracles*, illus. by Erika Weiks. Viking, 1991. ISBN 0-670-63047-X [25 p]. Fiction, Gr. K-4. **Disability: Blindness. (****) (Cat B)**

Hershel is a young boy who is blind. His mother is busily baking for the Jewish holiday Purim. Hershel wants to help but his mother says, "no." In a dream, an angel tells him he should make what he sees in his dreams. Hershel makes beautiful cookies and surprises his mother. They take the cookies to the market and every cookie is sold. Hershel is so happy because he has been a big help to his mother. The last two pages tell about the holiday Purim. This is a wonderful story that combines the beauty of the Jewish culture with the disability of blindness.

Themes or Units: **Children and Families Around the World; Holidays Around the World; Sight (seeing); Touch; We Are Alike, We Are Different.**

Greenfield, Eloise. *William and the Good Old Days,* **illus. by Jan Spivey Gilchrist. Harper Collins Publishers, 1993. ISBN 0-06-021093-1 [29 p]. Fiction, PS-2. Disability: Blindness, Physical (wheelchair). (****) (Cat C)**

This story is about a young boy who is African American. He is upset because his grandmother is ill and can no longer run her restaurant. He dreams about the good old days. Grandma can no longer see when she comes to live with her grandson's family. Still, they plan to plant the garden together and in the last illustration William is pushing Grandma in a wheelchair. This is a story that shows the genuine love between a grandson and grandmother.

Themes or Units: **Grandmothers and Grandfathers.**

Haines, Sandra. *Becca and Sue Make Two,* **illus. Gina Phillips. Writers Press, 1995. ISBN 1-885101-15-5 [32 p]. Fiction, K-3. Disability: Down Syndrome. (***) (Cat B)**

Becca learns about differences and understands that different people do things in different ways. She makes friends with Sue who has Down syndrome. Becca doesn't care that Sue learns more slowly or has some mannerisms different than her own. They are best friends. Together they learn to play a song on the piano for the recital which is a big success. This story promotes acceptance of persons with Down syndrome and uses the theme throughout that differences don't matter. In addition, the reader gains some information about Down syndrome.

Themes or Units: **Friendship; We Are Alike, We Are Different.**

Haldane, Suzanne. *Helping Hands: How Monkeys Assist People Who Are Disabled,* **photographs by author. Dutton Children's Books, 1991. ISBN 0-525-44723-7 [48 p]. Nonfiction, Gr. 3-7. Disability: Physical (wheelchair). (****) (Cat A)**

This book is a photo essay about Greg, a teenage boy with quadriplegia and his affectionate helper, Willie, a capuchin monkey. The story shows how the monkeys are trained to assist in everyday tasks such as opening a book or getting an item from the refrigerator. This assistance allows people with quadriplegia to become more self sufficient. The story shows what Greg can do with the help of his monkey. Children will enjoy seeing the many jobs Willie can do and how fun, yet tender he is with Greg. At the same time, they will learn what it's like to live with quadriplegia.

Themes or Units: **Pet Animals; We Are Alike, We Are Different; Zoo Animals.**

Hamm, Diane Johnson. *Grandma Drives a Motor Bed,* **illus. by Charles Robinson. Albert Whitman & Co., 1987. ISBN 0-8075-3025-5 [27 p]. Fiction, Gr. 1-3. Disability: Physical (wheelchair). (****) (Cat B)**

Josh and his mom visit Grandma who has a physical disability. Grandma is at home in a hospital bed most of the time and is able to sit in a wheelchair occasionally. Josh has many questions about how the bed works and why Grandma must be in it. He gets his questions answered and even has an opportunity to "try out" Grandma's bed. The story is very realistic and would answer many questions that children might have. While Grandma is limited in getting around, the story emphasizes all that she can do from her bed. The story promotes a positive attitude.

Themes or Units: **Dentists, Doctors, Nurses and Hospitals; Grandmothers and Grandfathers; Health.**

Hearn, Emily. *Franny and the Music Girl,* **illus. by Mark Thurman. Second Story Press, 1989. ISBN 0-929005-03-1 [22 p]. Fiction, Gr. PS-2. Disability: Physical (wheelchair). (****) (Cat C)**

Franny hears wonderful music floating down from the balcony above her apartment. She loves to listen and dance to the music. Others in the building complain about the noise so now Maia has no place to practice. Franny's family decides that during the day when Franny is at camp, Maia can use her room to practice. An upbeat story about "the music girl" and not about a disability. It promotes acceptance and respect by showing Franny participating in events like any other child.

Themes or Units: **Friendship; Homes and Neighborhoods; Sound (hearing).**

Hearn, Emily. *Good Morning Franny, Good Night Franny,* **illus. by Mark Thurman. The Women's Press, 1984. ISBN 0-88001-087-8 [30 p]. Fiction, Gr. PS-3. Disability: Physical (wheelchair). (****) (Cat C)**

Franny lives in the city and is thrilled that it's spring because now she can go for a walk with her friend. Ting sits on Franny's lap as they ride around the neighborhood and Franny helps Ting spell some words. Franny has to go to the hospital for tests and when she gets out her new friend has moved away. Franny is sad and goes to the park where she discovers Ting has painted a message to her on the sidewalk. This story emphasizes what Franny can do including antics in her wheelchair. It is about a friendship between two girls of different cultures and abilities.

Themes or Units: **Children and Families Around the World; City; Friendship; Safety; Spring; Transportation; Wheels; We Are Alike, We Are Different.**

Henriod, Lorraine. *Grandma's Wheelchair,* **pictures by Christa Chevalier. Albert Whitman and Co., 1982. ISBN 0807530352 [29 p]. Fiction, Gr. PS-2. Disability: Physical (wheelchair). (****) (Cat C)**

Each morning when Nate goes to kindergarten, his four-year-old brother Thomas goes to Grandma's house. Thomas's mom is about to have a baby so she has lost her lap, but Grandma always has a lap for him as she sits in her wheelchair. Grandma and Thomas keep very busy and have fun making apple sauce, vacuuming, dusting, and reading stories. This story clearly points out that a person with a disability can adapt to everyday life and function without losing independence. The illustrations and story promote a positive image of a person with a disability.

Themes or Units: **Families; Grandmothers & Grandfathers; Wheels; We Are Alike, We Are Different.**

Hesse, Karen. *Lester's Dog,* **illus. by Nancy Carpenter. Crown Publishers, Inc., 1993. ISBN 0-517-58357-7 [29 p]. Fiction, Gr. PS-3. Disability: Deafness. (****) (Cat C)**

A young boy sits on his front steps. Corey arrives and wants to show the young boy something up the hill. But, he is afraid of Lester's dog. Corey can't hear his friend's complaints because he is deaf. They pass Lester's house where his dog is busy digging and doesn't see them. Corey and his friend discover a little kitten and on the way back home the young boy overcomes his fears and yells at the dog. The words and beautiful illustrations capture the extraordinary friendship between these two boys. This story demonstrates natural inclusion and is an excellent story to promote acceptance and the attitude of "one of us."

Themes or Units: **Feelings (scared & angry); Friendship; Giving and Sharing; Pet Animals.**

Hines, Anna Grossnickle. *Gramma's Walk,* **illus. by author. Greenwillow Books, 1993. ISBN 0-688-11481-4 [28 p]. Fiction, Gr. PS-2. Disability: Physical (wheelchair). (****) (Cat C)**

Donnie visits his gramma who uses a wheelchair. During their visits they have a favorite activity of going on imaginary walks together. Today, they go to the seashore. During their imaginary outing, they see seagulls, deer tracks, boats, etc. The book is organized with the left page showing Donnie and his gramma talking and sharing, and the right page showing what they "see" on their outing. This is a story about their imagination, not about a disability. The story promotes a positive image of this grandmother who happens to be in a wheelchair.

Themes or Units: **Beach Party or Seashore; Grandmothers & Grandfathers.**

Holcomb, Nan. *Fair and Square,* **illus. by Dot Yoder. Jason & Nordic Publishers, 1992. ISBN 0-944727-09-3 [30 p]. Fiction, Gr. PS-1. Disability: Physical (use of switches). (***) (Cat B)**

Kevin is a young boy with a physical disability. He uses a wheelchair and has limited use of his hands. He wants to join in playing games with his family and friends but they keep telling him that it's too hard for him. In therapy, he learns how to use switches to run the computer and toy cars. Now he can play with his friends and be like everybody else. The story helps the reader see the importance of using switches to help persons with physical disabilities be more independent. The story promotes an attitude of "one of us."

Themes or Units: **Touch; We Are Alike, We Are Different.**

Holcomb, Nan. *Patrick and Emma Lou,* **illus. by Dot Yoder. Jason & Nordic Publishers, 1989. ISBN 0-944727-03-4 [30 p]. Fiction, Gr. PS-1. Disability: Physical (cerebral palsy, walker). (***) (Cat B)**

Patrick uses a wheelchair and Emma uses a walker. They are both at physical therapy on the same day. Patrick works on using a walker and Emma cheers him on. Emma is learning to walk with leg braces at the balance bars and Patrick cheers her on. At the end they go for a walk together both using their walkers. The author indicates that this book was written for children with physical disabilities. However, the story ends with a friendship developing between these two children which would be meaningful to children with or without disabilities.

Themes or Units: **Friendship; We Are Alike, We Are Different**

Holcomb, Nan. *Sarah's Surprise,* **illus. by Dot Yoder. Jason & Nordic Publishers, 1990. ISBN 0-944727-07-7 [32 p]. Fiction, PS-1. Disability: Speech/ Language. (**) (Cat B)**

Sarah uses a communication board. She wants to be able to sing Happy Birthday on her mom's birthday. The therapist surprises Sarah with a new Touch Talker that can say or sing whatever they program it to do. On her mom's birthday she presses the button and begins to "sing" Happy Birthday with everyone else. The story promotes an attitude of "one of us." One could question why Sarah does not use sign language to communicate since she has good use of her hands. In addition, the pencil sketchings have pink accents with only girls wearing pink. Few books are written about this disability.

Themes or Units: **Holidays (birthday); We Are Alike, We Are Different.**

Jordon, MaryKate. *Losing Uncle Tim,* **illus. by Judith Friedman. Albert Whitman & Co., 1989. ISBN 0-8075-4756-5 [32 p]. Fiction, Gr. K-3. Illness: AIDS. (****) (Cat B)**

Daniel is best friends with his Uncle Tim. Then, he discovers that Tim is very ill with AIDS. Daniel gets scared that he may catch AIDS but learns that you can't catch the disease by taking care of someone. This makes Daniel very happy and he continues to spend lots of time with Tim until he dies. Daniel is sad but remembers all that he has learned from his uncle. This is a sensitive story that provides children with accurate information about the possibility of catching AIDS and the emotional experience of having a loved one die.

Themes or Units: **Feelings; Friendship; Health.**

Karim, Roberta. *Mandy Sue Day*, **illus. by Karen Ritz. Clarion Books, 1994. ISBN 0-395-66155-2 [28 p]. Fiction, Gr. PS-3. Disability: Blindness. (****) (Cat C)**

Mandy has a day free of chores to choose whatever she wants to do. Mandy wants to spend her day with Ben, her horse and best friend. At bedtime she asks if she can sleep in the barn with Ben. As she gets ready to sleep in the loft, her brother gives her a flashlight. But, she reminds him she doesn't need it because she can't see. This is a beautiful example of inclusion. The story isn't about blindness rather about Mandy Sue's special day. The illustrations show the love between this girl and her horse.

Themes or Units: **Families; Farm and Farm Animals; Pet Animals; Sight (seeing); Summer; We Are Alike, We Are Different.**

Kastner, Jill. *Naomi knows It's Springtime*, **illus. by author. Boyd Mills Press, 1993. ISBN 1-56397-006-6 [32 p]. Fiction, Gr. PS-2. Disability: Blindness. (****) (Cat C)**

This is a story about Naomi who knows when spring arrives by hearing familiar sounds such as the squeaks of newborn birds. She smells the lilies and lilacs that bloom in her yard and serve as signs each year that winter is over and spring has arrived. The reader finds out on the last page of the story that Naomi is blind and can't see the blue sky that her neighbor sees. Naomi smiles and says, "If only Mrs. Jensen could see the rainbow in my mind." This is a very positive story showing Naomi enjoying a new season in her own special way. Exquisite, impressionist oil paintings help tell the story.

Themes or Units: **Sight (seeing); Smell; Sound (hearing); Spring; Touch; We Are Alike, We Are Different.**

Kornfield, Elizabeth J. *Dreams Come True*, **photographs by author. Rocky Mountain Children's Press, 1986. ISBN 0-940611-00-7 [24 p]. Nonfiction, Gr. 1-4. Disability/Illness: Epilepsy. (****) (Cat A)**

This is a delightful story about Katie whose dream is to be a figure skater like Dorothy Hamill. Katie has epilepsy. She explains what it's like to have a seizure, describes the tests, and talks about the medication she takes. Katie stresses that she can keep her dream of skating; having epilepsy doesn't mean she has to limit those dreams. This is a very informative and positive story about epilepsy and is supported by the Epilepsy Foundation of America. The story also helps create an image of "one of us" as Katie skates with her friends.

Themes or Units: **Health; Sports; We Are Alike, We Are Different.**

Krisher, Trudy. *Kathy's Hats: A Story of Hope*, illus. by Nadine Bernard Westcott. Albert Whitman & Co., 1992. ISBN 0-8075-4116-8 [29 p]. Fiction, Gr. PS-2. Illness: Cancer. (****) (Cat B)

This is moving story about a little girl who has cancer. For her, the worst time is when her hair falls out. She wears a baseball cap but doesn't like it. One day her mother tells her the most important hat of all is her thinking cap and how you feel about yourself. This is an excellent story as it shares the feelings that Kathy experiences with her treatments, yet it's a story with a positive ending. The story provides hope by pointing out that all cancer doesn't end in death. An excellent story for all young children to help alleviate their fears of cancer. In spite of the topic, it is an entertaining story.

Themes or Units: **Feelings; Friends & School; Hats; Health; We Are Alike, We Are Different.**

Kuklin, Susan. *Thinking Big: The Story of a Young Dwarf*, photographs by author. Lothrop, Lee & Shephard Books, 1986. ISBN 0-688-05826-4 [43 p]. Nonfiction, Gr. 2-5. Disability: Physical (dwarf). (****) (Cat B)

Jaime is smaller than her classmates because she is a dwarf. She is aware of her strengths and limitations and meets the challenges of everyday life with success because of her positive attitude and the support of her family. The story is written in a sensitive and caring style, however, "person first" language is not utilized. This is a well presented factual account of a child with a physical disability who demonstrates her competence in everyday activities.

Themes or Units: **Shapes and Sizes; We Are Alike, We Are Different.**

Lakin, Patricia. *Dad and Me In The Morning*, illus. by Robert G. Steele. Albert Whitman & Co., 1994. ISBN 0-8075-1419-5 [27 p]. Fiction, Gr. PS-2. Disability: Deafness. (****) (Cat C)

This story is about young Jacob and his father. Jacob gets up early, wakes his dad, and just the two of them hike to a special place to watch the morning sunrise. The illustrations capture the beautiful colors that appear during the spectacular sunrise. This is not a story about Jacob's deafness rather a story about a relationship between a father and a son. An excellent story that any child would enjoy.

Themes or Units: **Day and Night; Families; Ocean, Lakes & Rivers; Sight (seeing); Sounds (hearing).**

Lasker, Joe. *Nick Joins In*, illus. by author. Albert Whitman & Company, 1980. ISBN 0-8075-5612-2 [29 p]. Fiction, Gr. 2-3. Disability: Physical (leg braces and wheelchair). (***) (Cat B)

Nick is going to a new school and he's scared. He wonders what the kids will think when he can't walk or run. A teacher's aide meets him at the door and pushes him to his new classroom. The children ask lots of questions and then have fun working and playing with Nick. The story points out things that Nick can do as well as his limitations because of his need to use a wheelchair. He is accepted by his peers in this integrated setting. It would have strengthened the story if Nick had been allowed to maneuver his own wheelchair to the classroom demonstrating respect for what he can do.

Themes or Units: **Buildings; Feelings; Friends & School; Friendship; Transportation; Wheels; We Are Alike, We Are Different.**

Lee, Jeanne M. *Silent Lotus,* **illus. by author. Farrar, Straus & Giroux, 1991. ISBN 0-374-36911-9 [28 p]. Fiction, Gr. K-3. Disability: Deafness. (****) (Cat B)**

Lotus is a beautiful child who isn't able to speak. She is very sad and often by herself and lonely. Her parents know she cannot hear and see her unhappiness. They take her to the temple for a sign from the gods. Lotus sees the dancers and tries to copy their movements. She moves with grace and wants to learn to dance. The king and queen agree this is a sign. Lotus makes many friends, is no longer lonely and becomes the most famous dancer. This is a story from the Vietnamese culture and promotes a positive image of a person with blindness. Full page illustrations add to the story.
Themes or Units: **Feelings; Sports (dancing).**

Levi, Dorothy Hoffman. *A Very Special Friend,* **illus. by Ethel Gold. Kendall Green Publications, Gallaudet University Press, 1989. ISBN 0-930325-55-6 [28 p]. Fiction, Gr. K-3. Disability: Deafness. (****) (Cat B)**

One day Frannie gets excited as she sees a moving van at a house nearby. A family is moving in with a little girl her same age named Laura who is deaf and uses sign language. Frannie tells her mom that she cannot be friends because she can't understand Laura. Her mother explains that friends can talk to each other in many ways and often without words. Laura's mom helps Frannie understand some sign language and Frannie and Laura become special friends. This story promotes a positive image and the philosophy of "one of us" as Laura is accepted into her new neighborhood.
Themes or Units: **Feelings; Friendship; Homes and Neighborhoods; Sounds (hearing); Summer; We Are Alike, We Are Different.**

Levi, Dorothy Hoffman. *A Very Special Sister,* **illus. by Ethel Gold. Kendall Green Publications, 1992. ISBN 0-930323-96-3 [24 p]. Fiction, Gr. PS-2. Disability: Deafness. (****) (Cat B)**

Laura, who is deaf, is excited about becoming a sister. She shares the good news with her friends. Then, Laura begins to worry that the new baby will be able to hear and will be loved more than she. Laura goes on an outing with her mother who notices Laura's sadness. Suddenly, Laura cries and tells her mom of her worry. Her mother holds her and helps Laura understand her mom's love will never go away. A story that children will enjoy which promotes a positive image of a child with a hearing loss.
Themes or Units: **Brothers & Sisters; Friendship; Sounds (hearing); We Are Alike, We Are Different.**

Levine, Edna S. *Lisa and Her Soundless World*, illus. by Gloria Kamen. Human Sciences Press, 1974. ISBN 0-87705-104-6 [40 p]. Nonfiction, Gr. K-3. Disability: Deafness. (****) (Cat B)

This book does an outstanding job of discussing all of the senses and then explaining what it means to be deaf. When it looks like Lisa isn't hearing anything, her parents take her to a doctor. He tells the parents that Lisa needs a hearing aid and while she can't hear everything, she can hear some sounds for the first time. In addition, Lisa works on saying words, is learning how to lip read, and how to use sign language. This book contains accurate information, is very positive and would be an excellent book to explain deafness to young children. On the final pages, "person first" language is not used.
Themes or Units: Sound (hearing); We Are Alike, We Are Different.

Litchfield, Ada B. *A Button In Her Ear*, illus. by Eleanor Mill. Albert Whitman & Co., 1976. ISBN 0-8075-0987-6 [32 p]. Fiction, Gr. K-3. Disability: Hearing Loss. (****) (Cat B)

Angela has a mild hearing loss. She has her hearing checked by an audiologist and is fitted for a hearing aid. The next day, she can hear what everyone is saying. The teacher explains that just as she and several students wear glasses to see better, Angela wears an aid to hear better. The children hold the button close so they can hear. It is a magic button. The information is accurately and sensitively presented with Angela making humorous misinterpretations of what people are saying to her. The illustrations are a combination of pencil sketchings and colored pictures. This story promotes a "one of us" philosophy.
Themes or Units: Dentists, Doctors, Nurses and Hospitals; Friends and School; Sounds (hearing); We Are Alike, We Are Different.

Litchfield, Ada B. *Making Room for Uncle Joe*, illus. by Gail Owens. Albert Whitman & Co., 1984. ISBN 0-8075-4952-5 [26 p]. Fiction, Gr. 1-4. Disability: Down Syndrome. (***) (Cat B)

This story describes the adjustment and reactions of a family when their uncle with Down syndrome comes to live with them. Dan, a nephew, tells the story and explains how he worked through his own mixed feelings, how his little sister had almost immediate acceptance of Joe and how his older sister was angry and embarrassed. The story may promote some stereotypic behavior by persons with Down syndrome and does not utilize "person first" language. The author also refers to Down syndrome as Down's syndrome. Overall, this is a loving story of a family's acceptance of Uncle Joe.
Themes or Units: Families; Feelings; Giving and Sharing; We Are Alike, We Are Different.

Litchfield, Ada. *Words in Our Hands*, illus. by Helen Cogancherry. Albert Whitman & Co., 1980. ISBN 0-8075-9212-9 [29 p]. Fiction, Gr. K-3. Disability: Deafness. (***) (Cat A)

Michael, who is nine tells what it's like to live in a family when the mom and dad are both deaf. He explains how they communicate with sign language, lip reading and finger spelling. Examples of signing and finger spelling are included. He also shares how he feels when people stare or children make fun of his parents. It's a very helpful book for explaining deafness to young children. He points out the many things his parents can do which promotes a positive image.

Themes or Units: **Families; Sounds (hearing); We Are Alike, We Are Different.**

London, Jonathan. *The Lion Who Has Asthma*, illus. by Nadine Bernard Westcott. Albert Whitman & Co., 1992. ISBN 0-8075-4559-7 [24 p]. Fiction Gr. PS-2. Illness: Asthma (nebulizer). (****) (Cat B)

This is a story about a young boy with asthma. He pretends he's a lion but when it becomes difficult for him to breathe he doesn't feel like a lion anymore. His mom hooks him up to the nebulizer. During this time, he pretends the mask is there because he's piloting a plane. When he breathes easily again, he becomes the king of the jungle, the lion. This is an entertaining story with neat illustrations of the many animals in the jungle. All children would enjoy this story and learn about asthma too.

Themes or Units: **Health; Tools and Machines; Zoo Animals.**

Loski, Diana. *The Boy On The Bus*, illus. by Gina Phillips. Writer's Press Service, 1994. ISBN 1-885101-02-3 [30 p]. Nonfiction, Gr. 1-3. Disability: Attention Deficit Disorder (ADD). (****) (Cat B)

This story tells about all of the troubles Cory, who has ADD, has at school. One day he falls down and Margo, a classmate, walks him to the nurse's office. The nurse explains about ADD, the medication he takes and why Cory behaves like he does. The nurse tells Margo what Corey really needs is a friend. That day she saves a seat for him on the bus next to her. The explanation of ADD is very clear and appropriate for primary aged children. This is a good story about a topic that is difficult for children to understand.

Themes or Units: **Feelings; Friends and School; We Are Alike, We Are Different.**

Lyon, George Ella. *Cecil's Story*, illus. by Peter Catalanotto. Orchard Books, 1991. ISBN 0-531-05012-X [29 p]. Fiction, Gr. K-3. Disability: Physical (loss of limb). (****) (Cat C)

This story is about a boy whose father is in the Civil War. One day the boy's mother leaves to get his father while he stays with neighbors. He imagines what it would be like if his father didn't return and he'd have to take care of the animals and the plowing. He imagines what it would be like if his father is hurt in the fighting. His father returns with only one arm yet lifts the boy into an embrace. A very tender story with exquisite soft colored paintings that capture the emotions.

Themes or Units: **Families; Feelings; Peace Education.**

MacLachlan, Patricia. *Through Grandpa's Eyes,* **pictures by Deborah Kogan Ray. Harper Trophy, 1980. ISBN 0-06-443041-3 [37 p]. Fiction, Gr. K-3. Disability: Blindness. (****) (Cat B)**

John stays with his grandparents and does everything with his Grandpa who is blind. They exercise together, play the cello, go for walks and read books under the tree. John learns to see the world through his Grandpa's eyes including the smile in Grandmother's voice as she tells him to go to sleep at the end of a busy day. This story provides a positive image of a person who is blind by pointing out the many things that Grandpa can do and the loving relationship he has with his grandson. This is a sensitively written story with warm illustrations.

Themes or Units: **Families; Grandmothers and Grandfathers; Sight (hearing); Sounds (hearing); Smell; We Are Alike, We Are Different.**

Martin, Bill J.R. *Knots on a Counting Rope,* **illus. by Ted Rand. H. Holt, 1987. ISBN 0-0850-0571-4 [32 p]. Fiction, Gr. K-3. Disability: Blindness. (****) (Cat B)**

This is a story about a Native American boy and his grandfather. Using the story telling tradition, the grandfather tells the boy the story of his birth and how it left the child blind. The grandfather explains how the child deals with some of his struggles and fears. The counting rope is a metaphor for the passage of time and the boy's growing confidence. The warm illustrations add to this very sensitive and heartwarming story.

Themes or Units: **Children and Families Around the World; Families; Grandmothers and Grandfathers; Sight (seeing); We Are Alike, We Are Different.**

Mayer, Gina and Mercer. *A Very Special Critter,* **illus. by authors. Western Publishers, 1992. ISBN 0-307-12763-X [23 p]. Fiction, Gr. PS-3. Disability: Physical (wheelchair). (****) (Cat B)**

Alex is the new boy in class. The other children are curious because Alex is in a wheelchair. They have many questions and find out that Alex can do lots of things. He carries books in his pouches, plays volleyball and dresses up like a car for the Halloween party. What the children discover is that once in a while Alex needs help but so does everyone else. The book is an excellent example of inclusion and acceptance. The author emphasizes everything that Alex can do and being one of the gang is part of it.

Themes or Units: **Friends and School; We Are Alike, We Are Different.**

Merrifield, Margaret. *Come Sit By Me*, illus. by Heather Collins. Women's Press, 1990. ISBN 0-88961-141-6 [26 p]. Fiction, Gr. PS-3. Chronic Illness: HIV – AIDS. (****) (Cat B)

This is an educational book for young children and their caregivers about AIDS and HIV infection. Karen asks her mom, "What is AIDS?" Her mother explains and tells her that it is okay to play with Nicholas. Now other children won't play with Karen because she is playing with the boy with AIDS. Karen's parents organize a parent meeting where they talk about HIV and AIDS. Eventually all of the children play with Nicholas and call to him, "come sit by me." At the end, two pages outline ways you cannot get AIDS, and three pages provide information for parents, teachers, and caregivers.
Themes or Units: **Friends and School; Friendship; Health; We Are Alike, We Are Different; Colors in my World.**

Montoussamy-Ashe, Jeanne. *Daddy & Me*, photographs by author. Alfred A. Knopf, 1993. ISBN 0-679-85096-1 [34 p]. Nonfiction, Gr. PS-3. Chronic Illness: AIDS. (****) (Cat A)

This is a collection of black and white photographs with limited text that show the close relationship between a father who has AIDS and his young daughter. The photos show the many things they do together including going to the park, singing, and praying. She helps her daddy with his breathing machine much like he helps her when she is sick. While the reader knows the father has AIDS, the emphasis of this photo essay is on this loving father-daughter relationship that can still exist even when one is sick with a disease like AIDS.
Themes or Units: **Families; Health.**

Moon, Nicola. *Lucy's Picture*, illus. by Alex Ayliffe. Dial Books, 1994. ISBN 0-8037-1833-0 [24 p]. Fiction, Gr. PS-3. Disability: Blindness (guide dog). (****) (Cat C)

Lucy's grandfather is coming to school and she wants to surprise him. The other children are painting pictures, but she wants to make a collage. She collects many items including a clipping of her own hair. Grandpa who is blind is overwhelmed with her picture because he can feel the tree, bird and hair which is Honey his guidedog. The illustrations are extremely colorful and entertaining. All children would enjoy this story including the loving relationship between Lucy and her Grandpa.
Themes or Units: **Colors in My World; Giving and Sharing; Grandmothers and Grandfathers.**

Moran, George. *Imagine Me On A Sit-Ski!,* illus. by Nadine Bernard Westcott. Albert Whitman & Co., 1995. ISBN 0-8075-3618-0 [30 p]. Fiction, Gr. PS-3. Disability: Physical (cerebral palsy); Speech/Language (wordboard), Multiple (****) (Cat B)

Billy has cerebral palsy, uses a wheelchair and communicates using a word board. His class goes to the ski lodge to learn to ski. He uses a sit-ski while other students use a variety of other adapted ski equipment. It's an entertaining story showing persons with physical disabilities participating in a sport and having fun. The story is realistic and provides a positive image of persons with physical disabilities. This book would be a good choice during a unit on winter.

Themes or Units: **Sports; We Are Alike, We Are Different; Winter.**

Moss, Deborah M. *Lee, the Rabbit with Epilepsy,* illus. by Carol Schwartz. Woodbine House, 1989. ISBN 0-933149-32-8 [32 p]. Fiction, Gr. K-4. Disability/Illness: Epilepsy. (***) (Cat B)

This book uses animal characters to tell the story of Lee who has epilepsy. Lee's parents take her to the doctor who in simple terms describes the condition of epilepsy. The doctor prescribes some medication which will make the seizures go away. Lee is still worried about going places and doing things in case she has a seizure. Grandpa won't take "no" for an answer and takes Lee fishing where she gets a bite and catches a fish. "I knew you could do it," Grandpa says. The book provides accurate information about epilepsy through a story that is realistic, and reassuring.

Themes or Units: **Dentists, Doctors, Nurses & Hospitals; Families; Fish; Grandmothers & Grandfathers; Health; Summer (fishing); We Are Alike, We Are Different.**

Moss, Deborah M. *Shelley The Hyperactive Turtle,* illus. by Carol Schwartz. Woodbine House, 1989. ISBN 0-933149-31-X [19 p]. Fiction, Gr. K-3. Disability/Illness: Hyperactivity. (**) (Cat B)

Animal characters are used to tell the story of a turtle who is hyperactive. Shelley doesn't have friends and feels sad because everyone thinks he is bad. The doctor diagnoses his problem as hyperactivity. Shelley goes to a therapist each week and takes a pill every morning to help calm down. The story emphasizes all of the troubles that Shelley experiences. After Shelley receives help, the story quickly ends which limits the opportunity of providing a positive image of Shelley. It's important that children understand that the child is responsible for his or her behavior not the medication.

Themes or Units: **Dentist, Doctor, Nurses, and Hospitals; Health; We Are Alike; We Are Different.**

Muldoon, Kathleen M. *Princess Pooh*, illus. by Linda Shute. Albert Whitman & Co., 1989. ISBN 0-8075-6627-6 [29 p]. Fiction, Gr. 2-5. Disability: Physical (crutches, wheelchair). (****) (Cat B)
Patty calls her sister Princess Pooh because she sits on her throne on wheels. When Penny is sleeping, Patty takes off in her wheelchair. Patty falls out of the chair cutting her knee. She crosses a street but only makes it to the middle when the light changes. Patty is sure she is going to get hit. Many other things happen like people looking at her and turning away. Finally she gets off the chair and pushes it home. Patty has a new understanding of her sister. This is an excellent story to help children understand the challenges of having a disability and using a wheelchair.
Themes or Units: **Brothers and Sisters; Feelings; Transportation.**

Muller, Gerda. *The Garden In The City*, illus. by author. Dutton Children's Books, 1992. ISBN 0-525-44697-4 [36 p]. Fiction, Gr. 1-4. Disability: Physical (wheel chair). (****) (Cat C)
Ben and Caroline, children who live in the city in the same apartment building, decide to have a garden. This story goes through their planning and making the garden. Other friends join in, including one friend who is in a wheelchair. The children come up with innovations that make it possible for him to participate in planting and harvesting. Throughout the story readers learn facts about identifying, growing and caring for a variety of plants. The illustrations are outstanding. Children would have hours of fun looking at the pictures.
Themes or Units: **Homes & Neighborhoods; Planting & Gardening; Spring.**

Newth, Philip. *Roly Goes Exploring*. Philomel Books, 1981. ISBN 3-0102-00335-2208 [21 p]. Fiction, Gr. PS-2. Disability: Blindness (Braille). (***) (Cat C)
Roly is a small circle. This story is about Roly's adventures after he leaves his friends. During his trip, he finds rectangles, triangles, squares and half circles. He finds shapes that are big and little. He finds shapes that don't belong because they are different. He returns to his friends with a new friend, a big circle. This story is for children who are blind or sighted as the story is presented in braille and standard type. The pictures of the variety of shapes are cut outs to feel as well as see. The final page of the book provides information about braille type. This story is about shapes and the sense of touch.
Themes or Units: **Shapes and Sizes; Counting; Sight (seeing); Touch; We Are Alike, We Are Different.**

O'Shaughnessy, Ellen. *Somebody Called Me A Retard Today...and My Heart Felt Sad,* illus. by David Garner. Walker & Co., 1992. ISBN 0-8027-8196-9 [18 p]. Nonfiction, Gr. PS-K. Disability: Mental Retardation, Learning Disability. (****) (Cat A)

This is a short story that describes how a child feels when called a "retard." The father talks to the child stressing the child's positive characteristics including all of the things the child can do. This is a good story to promote discussion about name calling because the story points out how the recipient feels. The story could be used for any name calling whether or not it's related to having a disability. The child in the illustrations could be a girl or a boy which may increase the story's use.

Themes or Units: **Feelings; We Are Alike, We Are Different.**

Osofsky, Audrey. *My Buddy,* illus. by Ted Rand. Henry Hold & Co., 1992. ISBN 0-8050-1747-X [28 p]. Fiction, Gr. PS-3. Disability: Physical (muscular dystrophy, wheelchair). (****) (Cat A)

This is a heartwarming story about a young boy who has muscular dystrophy and his dog. Buddy has been trained to do things that the boy cannot do for himself such as turning on light switches and picking up items. Once trained, Buddy helps his master at the pet store, at school, at a friend's house and even when the boy is playing T-ball. Children will be amazed at all the things Buddy can do for his master. The story stresses the independence the young boy has because of Buddy. The colorful illustrations capture the acceptance of this boy and his dog and the love between them.

Themes or Units: **Pet Animals; We Are Alike, We Are Different.**

Pearson, Susan. *Happy Birthday, Grampie,* pictures by Ronald Himler. Dial Books, 1987. ISBN 0-8037-3458-1 [27 p]. Fiction, Gr. PS-3. Disability: Blindness. (****) (Cat C)

Martha makes a special birthday card for her Grampa who is blind. At the nursing home, they give a birthday party for Grampa. After Martha gives him her card, Grandpa concentrates on feeling the raised letters which say "I love you." Suddenly, Grandpa's face lights up, he gives Martha a big hug and says, "Martha, I love you too." The story is realistic considering that Grandpa is 89 years old. The feelings of love and respect exist for the young and the old, with or without a disability.

Themes or Units: **Children and Families Around the World; Dentist, Doctors, Nurses & Hospitals (nursing home); Families; Feelings; Grandmothers & Grandfathers; Giving & Sharing; Sight (seeing); Touch.**

Peckinpah, Sandra Lee. *Chester...The Imperfect All-Star*, illus. by Trisha Moore. Dasan Publishing, 1993. ISBN 0-9627806-1-8 [37 p]. Fiction, Gr. 1-3. Disability: Physical (one leg shorter; prosthesis). (**) (Cat B)

This is a story of a young boy's dream and determination to play baseball even though he has a disability. The story begins as a fairy tale and ends as a real baseball game. The coach tapes a broken bat to Chester's leg so he can run like everyone else. Chester helps the team win the game by hitting a home run. It's unfortunate that the word "imperfect" was selected as part of the title. This leads to stereotypic thinking (i.e. someone is imperfect if a body part is different). The story also depicts Chester as hitting a home run and winning the ball game. Does Chester have to be "super hero" in order to be accepted?

Themes or Units: **Sports; We Are Alike, We Are Different.**

Peckinpah, Sandra Lee. *Rosey...the imperfect angel*, illus. by Trisha Moore. Scholars Press, 1991. ISBN 0-9627806-0-X [25 p]. Fiction, Gr. 1-3. Disability: Speech/Language (cleft lip). (***) (Cat B)

This is a fairy tale about Rosey, a young angel with a cleft lip. In the Land Above, Rosey's peer angels taunt her. With the support of the Boss Angel, Rosie is given the Garden of January where she works and ultimately grows the most beautiful flowers. Rosey is then sent to the Land Below where a new baby was born with a cleft lip. Rosey is to teach the family about the beauty of imperfection. The author has written a delightful fairy tale about a difficult topic. The illustrations are realistic, yet pleasing.

Themes or Units: **Feelings; Planting and Gardening; We Are Alike, We Are Different.**

Peterson, Jeanne Whitehouse. *I Have A Sister My Sister Is Deaf*, pictures by Deborah Kogan Ray. Harper Trophy, 1984. ISBN 0-06-443059-6 [32 p]. Fiction, Gr. PS-3. Disability: Deafness. (****) (Cat A)

A young girl describes what life is like for her little sister who is deaf. She explains that being deaf doesn't hurt, although her sister's feelings are hurt when people don't understand. While her sister may be limited with the words she can speak, she can say more with facial expressions than most people can with words. The information presented is realistic and emphasizes abilities as well as limitations. The story and the pencil sketched illustrations portray a sister's loving relationship with her little sister. The story is written with simplicity and sensitivity and helps the reader enter the world of a person who has total deafness.

Themes or Units: **Brothers & Sisters; Families; Sounds (hearing); We Are Alike, We Are different.**

Pirner, Connie White. *Even Little Kids Get Diabetes,* **pictures by Nadine Bernard Wescott. Albert Whitman & Co., 1991. ISBN 0-8075-2158-2 [21 p]. Nonfiction, Gr. PS-2. Illness: Diabetes. (****) (Cat A)**

The story is about a girl who gets diabetes when she is two years old. The story is very positive with the emphasis on eating the right foods at the right times, having finger pokes and shots so she doesn't get sick. The story also addresses the feelings that other members of the family have as they worry about the disease. This story would help young children understand the illness of diabetes and why the person isn't allowed to eat sweets and needs to have insulin shots in order to be healthy. The illustrations are very colorful.

Themes or Units: Dentists, Doctors, Nurses and Hospitals; Health; We Are Alike; We Are Different.

Porte, Barbara Ann. *Harry's Dog,* **illus. by Yossi Abolafia. Greenwillow Books, 1984. ISBN 0-6880-02555-2 [47 p]. Fiction, Gr. K-3. Illness: Allergies. (****) (Cat B)**

Harry wants a dog so badly but he can't because his Dad is allergic to dogs. So, Harry sneaks a dog into his room. When he is found out, Harry proceeds to tell three farfetched stories as to how he got the dog and why it can't be returned. His Dad understands because when he was growing up he wanted one too, but couldn't because of his allergies. An aunt comes to the rescue agreeing to keep Harry's dog. This is an entertaining story that would help children have a better understanding about allergies. This book is like an early reader with an illustration and 4 to 6 sentences on each page.

Themes or Units: Health; Pet Animals.

Powers, Mary Ellen. *Our Teacher's in a Wheelchair,* **pictures by author. Albert Whitman & Company, 1986. ISBN 0-8075-6240-8 [20 p]. Nonfiction, Gr. PS-3. Disability: Physical (wheelchair). (****) (Cat A)**

Brian is a teacher in a child-care center. While in college he had an accident playing lacrosse which paralyzed his legs and necessitates his using a wheelchair. Black and white photographs show Brian at home as well as working with the children. The story points out all that Brian can do as well as some of the difficulties he encounters. Children need to realize that some of the difficulties are due to the environment (i.e. curbs). The story illustrates that while Brian may need help at times, everyone does. The story is very realistic and sensitively written.

Theme or Units: **Health; Safety; Feelings; Wheels; Community Helpers (teacher); Transportation; We Are Alike-We Are Different.**

Quinlan, Patricia. *Tiger Flowers*, **illus. by Janet Wilson. Dial Books, 1994. ISBN 0-8037-1407-6 [29 p]. Fiction, Gr. K-3. Illness: AIDS. (****) (Cat B)**
Joel has a special uncle, Michael. Together they go to baseball games and build a treehouse. Joel becomes even closer to his uncle when he comes to live with Joel's family because he has AIDS. When his uncle dies, Joel finds comfort in the many happy memories of his uncle. At the end of the story, Joel gives his sister a Tiger Flower which was his uncle's favorite flower and now has become Joel's favorite flower too. This is an outstanding story to help children learn about AIDS because it is realistic yet so caring. Vibrant illustrations highlight this story.
Themes or Units: **Families; Health**

Rabe, Berniece. *The Balancing Girl*, **illus. by Lillian Hoban. E.P. Dutton, 1981. ISBN 0-525-44364-9 [32 p]. Fiction, Gr. K-3. Disability: Physical (wheelchair, leg braces, crutches). (****) (Cat C)**
At school, Margaret is so good at balancing things that she is called "The Balancing Girl." Tommy gives Margaret a hard time about all of her balancing activities by belittling and trying to destroy her efforts. Then, the principal asks the children for ideas for booths at the school carnival. Margaret's idea brings in the most money. The story promotes a positive image of a person with a disability and clearly shows Margaret participating in the activities that take place. It promotes a "one of us" attitude.
Themes or Units: Colors in my World (red); Friends & School; Friendship; Transportation; Wheels; We Are Alike, We Are Different.

Rabe, Berniece. *Where's Chimpy?*, **photographs by Diane Schmidt. Albert Whitman & Co., 1988. ISBN 0-8075-8928-4 [26 p]. Nonfiction, Gr. PS-2. Disability: Down Syndrome. (****) (Cat C)**
Misty is in bed with dad ready to read a story when she realizes she doesn't have Chimpy, her bedtime monkey. They go back through her day looking for the monkey. Everywhere they find something that Misty has left behind. When Chimpy is found, Dad reads a story but before going to sleep, they count the newly found toys. The colored photographs capture the warm relationship between Misty and her Daddy. The re-creation of the day's activities points out that Misty goes places, plays with toys and likes similar things to any other young child. Any child would enjoy this outstanding book.
Themes or Units: Families; Naptime and Bedtime; Numbers in My Everyday World; We Are Alike, We Are Different.

Raffi. One Light, One Sun, illus. by Eugenie Fernandes. Crown Publishers, Inc., 1988. ISBN 0-517-56785-7 [29 p]. Fiction, Gr. PS-2. Disability: Physical (wheelchair). (****) (Cat C)
This story points out how one sun lights everyone's day. The sun shines on families from three houses as they play and picnic by the stream. As the sun goes down all of the families go home to eat dinner, do activities, and then go to bed. As the sun comes up, the families awaken for another day. One family has a child in a wheelchair. The story shows that his routines are similar to the children in the other houses which promotes a "one of us" attitude.
Themes or Units: **Beach Party; Buildings; Colors in my World; Day & Night; Families; Homes & Neighborhoods; Naptime & Bedtime; Picnics; Summer.**

Rankin, Laura. *The Handmade Alphabet,* **illus. by author. Dial Books, 1991. ISBN 0-8037-0975-7 [27 p]. Nonfiction, All ages. Disability: Deafness. (****) (Cat A)**

This book introduces the visual world of signing utilizing American Sign Language. Each page illustrates a handshape for the manual alphabet and a corresponding letter of the written alphabet. A picture of an item that begins with that letter is shown with the signing hand. For example, the hand that signs "V" holds a valentine; the hand signing "R" is entwined with a ribbon. The illustrations are very realistic depicting hands of male and female as well as the young and old. Children would need some understanding of signing before this book would be of interest.
Themes or Units: **Sight (seeing); Sounds (hearing); We Are Alike, We Are Different.**

Rogers, Alison. *Luke Has Asthma, Too,* **illus. by Michael Middleton. Waterfront Books, 1987. ISBN 0-914525-06-9 [31 p]. Nonfiction, Gr. PS-2. Illness: Asthma. (****) (Cat B)**

This is a story about a boy who has asthma. He looks up to Luke because he has asthma and still plays baseball and rides his bike. The story explains what it feels like to have asthma and shows the machines and inhalers that are used. When his asthma gets really bad he has to go to the hospital. He and his dad learn new exercises to do when he has trouble breathing. When he returns home, Luke brings him a baseball cap just like his and they ride their bikes. This story demonstrates respect for the child with asthma and stresses what he can do. It provides accurate information and promotes a positive image.
Themes or Units: **Friendship; Giving and Sharing; Hats; Health.**

Rosenberg, Maxine B. *Finding A Way: Living with Exceptional Brothers and Sisters,* **photographs by George Ancone. Lothrop, Lee & Shepard Books, 1988. ISBN 0-688-06874-X [45 p]. Nonfiction, Gr. K-3. Disability/Illness: Diabetes, Asthma, & Spina Bifida. (****) (Cat B)**

This story explores the feelings of siblings from three different families who have a child with a disability or chronic illness. The siblings feelings are openly discussed as are the many good times they have with their brother or sister. The story is honest and realistic and describes many of the daily routines which occur in families. This story promotes a positive image by emphasizing what these children can do as well as the challenges they encounter. This book may help brothers and sisters understand and work through the feelings they experience. The author does not use "person first" language.
Themes or Units: **Brothers & Sisters; Families; Feelings; Health; We Are Alike, We Are Different.**

Rosenberg, Maxine B. *My Friend Leslie: The Story of a Handicapped Child*, photographs by George Ancona. Lothrop, Lee & Shephard Books, 1983. ISBN 0-688-01690-1 [43 p]. Nonfiction, Gr. K-3. Disability: Multiple Disabilities – Visual, Hearing Loss, Cleft Palate and Muscular Imperfection. (****) (Cat A)

Karin describes her friendship with Leslie who was born with multiple disabilities. The story realistically describes Leslie's disabilities and the resulting frustrations. However, the fun times, the joy of friendship, and Leslie's delightful personality are equally portrayed. Black and white photographs represent cultural diversity and make the book even more outstanding. This story promotes a positive image of a child with multiple disabilities by emphasizing her independence, success in the mainstream, and her exuberant friendship. Except for the title, the story does use "person first" language.

Themes or Units: Friends and School; Friendship; Sight (seeing); Sounds (hearing); We Are Alike, We Are Different.

Russo, Marisabina. *Alex Is My Friend*, illus. by author. Greenwillow Books, 1992. ISBN 0-688-10419-5 [30 p]. Fiction, Gr. PS-2. Disability: Physical (inhibited growth in stature). (****) (Cat B)

Alex and Ben are friends. As they grow older, Ben wonders why Alex isn't bigger because he's a year older. His mom explains that Alex will always remain small. Ben soon realizes that Alex's size doesn't really matter and their friendship continues to grow. A delightful story which emphasizes that differences don't really matter. Colorful illustrations similar to folk art accompany the story.

Themes or Units: Body Awareness; Friendship; Giving and Sharing; We Are Alike, We Are Different.

Sanford, Doris. *David Has AIDS*, illus. by Graci Evans. Multnomah Press, 1989. ISBN 0-88070-299-0 [26 p]. Nonfiction, Gr. K-2. Illness: AIDS. (****) (Cat B)

This story is about David, a young boy who has AIDS and eventually dies. Throughout the story David says prayers to God to help him. The story teaches children about AIDS and about death. It has a limited text with soft, tender illustrations. A very sensitive and loving story.

Themes or Units: Friendship; Health.

Sanford, Doris. *Don't Look at Me*, illus. by Graci Evans. Multnomah Press, 1986. ISBN 0-88070-150-1 [24 p]. Fiction, Gr. 1-3. Disability: Mental Retardation or Learning Disability. (****) (Cat A)

This story is about Patrick who has a difficult time learning and thinks he is dumb. The story is an effort to help Patrick see that it's his attitude and how he thinks about himself that is important. His pet lamb and his grandfather help him understand his feelings and what he can do to feel better about himself. This is a heartwarming story that would help children understand their own or others feelings when learning is difficult. The illustrations do an exceptional job of portraying the mood and feelings of the characters.

Themes or Units: Feelings; Friends & School, We Are Alike, We Are Different.

Sanford, Doris. *Help! Fire!*, Illus. by Graci Evans. Multnomah Press, 1992. ISBN 0-88070-520-5 [30 p]. Fiction, Gr. K-3. Disability: Physical (legs below the knee are missing). (****) (Cat B)

Daniel is a young boy who doesn't have legs below his knees. One day, Daniel is home because he doesn't feel well. A neighborhood youngster falls outside their house so his mom and brother take him home. While they are gone, a fire starts. Daniel is frightened and calls 911. Daniel and his two dogs make it to the patio but can't go any further. The firesquad rescues them. The story does an excellent job of showing all the things Daniel can do even with his physical disability. It's an exciting story that all children would love with colorful illustrations.

Themes or Units: Community Workers; Pet Animals; Safety; We Are Alike, We Are Different.

Sargent, Susan & Wirt, Donna Aaron. *My Favorite Place*, illus. by Allan Eitzen. Abingdon Press, 1983. ISBN 0-687-27538-5 [27 p]. Fiction, Gr. PS-3. Disability: Blindness. (****) (Cat C)

A little girl goes to the ocean with her mom and dad. She helps lay out the blanket, swims in the ocean, goes for a walk, and takes a nap on the beach. Throughout the story she comments on things she smells, hears or feels. It isn't until the end of the story that the reader finds out that she is blind. The story promotes a positive image as this little girl fully participates in the day's activities and enjoys the outing. The beach is her favorite place.

Themes or Units: Beach Party or Seashore; Oceans, Lakes and Rivers; Sight (seeing); Smell; Sound (hearing); Summer; Taste; Touch.

Seuling, Barbara. *I'm Not So Different*, illus. Pat Schories. Western Publishing Co., 1986. ISBN 0-307-62486-2 [22 p]. Fiction, Gr. K-3. Disability: Physical (wheelchair). (****) (Cat B)

Kit is a young girl who uses a wheelchair. When she complains about being different, her dad points out how everyone has differences which don't have to stop a person from being good at lots of things. At the end of the concert, the rock star talks to Kit. She is excited as she says to her dad, "You're right. I'm not so different." The story promotes a positive image of a person using a wheelchair. The story takes place in integrated settings, i.e. school and community. "Person first" language is not always used.

Themes or Units: Families; Friendship; Giving and Sharing; We Are Alike, We Are Different.

Silverstein, A. Ivin, & Silverstein, Virginia B. *Runaway Sugar: All About Diabetes*, illus. Harriett Barton. J. B. Lippincott, 1981. ISBN 0-397-31928-2 [32 p]. Nonfiction, Gr. 1-3. Illness: Diabetes. (***) (Cat A)

This book explains the causes of diabetes and what happens in the body when a person has this disease. The danger signs are outlined and the process of taking insulin fully discussed. The book provides current, factual information regarding diabetes. However, the amount of information may be somewhat overwhelming and may need to be presented over time. The information provided does not address the emotional side of having diabetes such as pointing out a child's ability to fully participate in activities like any other child, and the feelings associated with having this disease and injecting with insulin.
Themes or Units: **Health.**

Simpson-Smith, Elizabeth. *A Guide Dog Goes to School*, illus. by Bert Dobson. William Morrow & Co., 1987. ISBN 0-688-06844-8 [47 p]. Nonfiction, Gr. 1-3. Disability: Blindness. (****) (Cat A)

A golden retriever called Cinderella is selected to go to guide school. The story takes the reader through the entire training process and a month's training with the person who is blind and will become its master. While the story is very informative, it is also very entertaining. The reader grows to love Cinderella. Pencil sketches capture the feelings of joy between Cinderella and her new master. This story would interest young children and provide important information about persons who are blind, how they use dogs to guide them and, how the dog becomes a pet when it isn't working.
Themes or Units: **Pet Animals; Sight (seeing).**

Slier, Debby. *Animal Signs: A First Book of Sign Language.* Checkerboard Press, 1993. ISBN 1-56288-385-2 [14 p]. Nonfiction, PS-K. Disability: Hearing Loss, Deafness (signing). (****) (Cat A)

This book contains 14 colored photographs of common animals. Each page contains a photograph with a small inset of a child demonstrating the appropriate sign. The insets are black and white sketches of boys and girls from diverse cultures using American Sign Language. Signing is usually used by persons who are deaf or have a hearing loss, however, this book emphasizes that any child can benefit from using sign language and can have fun using it. The pages are made of hardboard which makes the book durable for younger children and may make turning pages easier for some children.
Themes or Units: **Farm and Farm Animals; Sight (seeing); Sound (hearing).**

Slier, Debby. *Word Signs: A First Book of Sign Language.* **Checkerboard Press, 1993. ISBN 1-56288-386-0 [14 p]. Nonfiction, PS-K. Disability: Hearing Loss, Deafness (signing). (****) (Cat A)**
Each page contains a colored photograph of a common object (e.g. socks, crayons, baby). Each photograph has a small inset of a child demonstrating the appropriate sign for the object. The insets are sketches of boys and girls from diverse cultures using American Sign Language. The book emphasizes that any child can benefit from using sign language and can enjoy using it. This is an excellent book for beginning signing for young children. The pages are made of hardboard which makes them durable for younger children and may make it easier for some children to turn the pages.
Themes or Units: **Sight (seeing); Sound (hearing).**

Swanson, Susanne M. *My Friend Emily,* **illus. by Paul Hart. Writer's Press Service, 1994. ISBN 1-885101-04-X [35 p]. Nonfiction, Gr. 1-3. Disability/Illness: Epilepsy. (****) (Cat B)**
This story is about two young girls who are best friends. Emily has epilepsy. The story does an outstanding job of explaining about epilepsy and describing seizures. The story emphasizes that Emily is like any other child except for the seizures. The story also promotes cultural diversity as the best friends represent two different cultures.
Themes or Units: **Friendship; Health; We Are Alike, We Are Different.**

Taylor, Ron. *All by Self,* **illus. by Jay Jacoby. Light On Books & Videotapes, 1991. ISBN 0-938991-75-2 [64 p]. Nonfiction, Gr. K-6. Disability: Cerebral Palsy (wheelchair). (****) (Cat A)**
A father speaks with simplicity and sensitivity about his son who has cerebral palsy. The story describes how a family deals with the questions that can never be answered and the grieving for what will never be. It also portrays the powerful, loving relationship between this father and his child. Through the use of beautiful pencil sketchings and poetic language, Micah's father emphasizes the mutual teaching and learning he experiences with his son and the wonder and joy of discovery. This is a well written story about Micah's journey that is filled with love.
Themes or Units: **Families; Feelings; We Are Alike, We Are Different.**

Thompson, Mary. *My Brother Matthew,* **illus. by author. Woodbine House, 1992. ISBN 0-933149-47-6 [25 p]. Fiction, Gr. K-3. Disability: Physical and Speech/Language Delay (brain injury). (****) (Cat B)**
David tells what it is like to be the older brother of Matthew who was born with a brain injury. When a child with a disability is born into a family, sometimes life can shift to center around that child. Sisters and brothers can feel scared and left out. When Matthew comes home from the hospital, David interacts and enjoys playing with him. As Matthew grows older, David realizes how much they are alike even if Matthew talks and moves differently. David describes some of his feelings as he lives with his brother. The story includes many things Matthew can do and the fun the two brothers have together.
Themes or Units: **Families; Brothers & Sisters; Feelings; Grandmothers & Grandfathers; We Are Alike, We Are Different.**

Verniero, Joan C. *You Can Call Me Willy*, illus. by Verdon Flory. Magination Press, 1995. ISBN 0-945354-60-6 [27 p]. Fiction, Gr. 1-4. Illness: HIV infection and AIDS. (****) (Cat B)

Willy has the HIV virus. She got it from her mother when she was born. Her grandmother had to attend meetings before Willy could begin school because other parents had concerns that their children would get the infection, too. Some parents were worried about her playing on the baseball team too, but all of the problems were worked out. From this story children would learn the facts about getting HIV. They would also find out how it feels to have this disease. The illustrations show diverse cultures; Willy is African American.

Themes or Units: **Feelings; Friends and School; Health; We Are Alike, We Are Different.**

Wahl, Jan. *Jamie's Tiger*, illus. by Tomie de Paola. Harcourt Brace Jovanovich, 1978. ISBN 0-15-239500-8 [40 p]. Fiction, Gr. PS-3. Disability: Hearing Loss. (****) (Cat B)

Jamie develops a hearing loss and is frightened about what is happening to him until the doctor discusses his hearing loss. Someone from school teaches him to lip read, hand talk and finger spell. Jamie grows lonely until old friends begin to learn how to finger spell and discover it isn't so hard and it can be their secret code. The illustrations show the emotions of sadness changing to happiness as he interacts with his friends. The story promotes an attitude of "one of us" as it shows that a hearing loss can happen to anyone and you can still be friends.

Themes or Units: **Friendship; Sound (hearing); We Are Alike, We Are Different.**

Whinston, Joan Lenett. *I'm Joshua & Yes I Can*, illus. by Wally Littman. Vantage Press, 1989. ISBN 0-533-07959-4 [34 p]. Fiction, Gr. 3-6. Disability: Cerebral Palsy (leg braces). (****) (Cat B)

This story centers around Joshua's first day in first grade and his fears about children who might make fun of him because he has cerebral palsy. He realizes that although there are things he cannot do, he does have special talents. With courage and determination he deals with his limitations and the awkward moments and regains confidence in himself and his abilities. This story promotes acceptance and an attitude of "one of us" as it addresses both Joshua's challenges and his abilities. Cartoon like illustrations accompany the story.

Themes or Units: **Feelings; Friends & School; We Are Alike, We Are Different.**

White, Paul. *Janet at School*, photographs by Jeremy Finlay. Thomas Y. Crowell, Co., 1978. ISBN 0-381-99556-9 [23 p]. Nonfiction, Gr. PS-2. Disability: Physical, Spina Bifida (leg braces & wheelchair). (****) (Cat B)

Janet is a five-year-old with spina bifida who attends school in a mainstream classroom. The story provides an account of her daily routines and the adaptations that are utilized so that Janet can be independent. The story also provides a clear explanation of spina bifida that young children would be able to understand. This story emphasizes many things that Janet can do as well as her limitations and describes how she is included in her family's outings. The color photographs add to the story.

Themes or Units: **Families; We Are Alike, We Are Different.**

Wiener, Lori S., Best, Aprille, & Pizzo, Phillip A (Eds.). *Be A Friend: Children Who Live with HIV Speak*, illus. by children with HIV. Albert Whitman & Co., 1994. ISBN 0-8075-0590-0 [40 p]. Nonfiction, Gr. All Ages. Illness: HIV and AIDS. (****) (Cat A)

Children from five to fifteen years of age tell what it is like to live with HIV infection and AIDS. The children's writings and art work are included in this collection. They talk about being scared, how people treat them, about dying and many other emotions. This book would help children learn about the facts of this disease, but in addition, the children's letters would help them learn about the emotional aspects that are so difficult to live with. This book promotes understanding and empathy regarding AIDS.

Themes or Units: **Feelings; Health.**

Wright, Betty Ren. *My Sister Is Different*, illus. by Helen Cogancherry. Raintree Steck-Vaughn, 1992. ISBN 0-8172-1369-4 [28 p]. Fiction, Gr. K-3. Disability: Mental Retardation. (****) (Cat B)

Carlo has an older sister who has mental retardation. He tells how difficult it is when he has to watch her. It isn't until he loses her in a department store that he thinks about all the good things she does such as making the baby laugh and happily helping with dishes. When Carlo finds Terry, he begins to appreciate her for who she is and doesn't mind looking after her. The story is very realistic regarding feelings that siblings have toward their brother or sister with a disability. It is sensitively written, respectful and has colorful illustrations that capture the many emotions that are experienced.

Themes or Units: **Brothers & Sisters; We Are Alike, We Are Different.**

Wright, Christine. *Just Like Emma: How She Has Fun in God's World*, illus. by Biz Hull. Augsburg Fortress Publishers, 1993. ISBN 0-8066-2617-8 [26 p]. Nonfiction, Gr. K-3. Disability: Physical (Spina Bifida). (****) (Cat B)

This is a story about Emma who has spina bifida. She lives with her father and younger brother. Throughout the story Emma participates in household tasks such as drying the dishes and making out the grocery list. Humor is incorporated into the story when she and her brother put crushed chips into the cereal box for their dad's breakfast. Emma even goes swimming with her family and out smarts her brother. The emphasis in this story is what Emma can do for herself and with her family. This is a very positive yet realistic story. The illustrations are colorful, and very life like.

Themes or Units: **Brothers and Sisters; Families; We Are Alike, We Are Different.**

Zelonsky, Joy. *I Can't Always Hear You,* **illus. by Barbara Bejna & Shirlee Jensen. Raintree Steck-Vaughn, 1991. ISBN 0-8172-1355-4 [30 p]. Fiction, Gr. K-3. Disability: Hearing Loss (hearing aids). (****) (Cat B)**

Kim begins school in an integrated class at a new building where she doesn't know anyone. She has a hearing loss, wears a hearing aid and worries about being different. With the help of her teacher and new classmates she soon realizes that everyone has individual differences (i.e. one student wears braces, one is adopted, another is very tall). A very realistic story about differences that promotes a positive image of a person with a hearing loss. The story also promotes cultural diversity; a teacher and student are African American and Kim is Asian.

Themes or Units: **Friends and School; Sounds; We Are Alike, We Are Different.**

CHAPTER SEVEN

Children's Books Cross-Referenced by Disability or Chronic Illness

Introduction

The books in this selection have been cross-referenced by disability or chronic illness. In the event that a book contains information about more than one disability or illness, it is cross-referenced for all that are present. This list includes books for nine disability areas: autism, blind, low vision and partially sighted, deaf and hearing impaired, emotional and behavioral disorders (includes ADHD), learning disability, mental retardation (includes Down syndrome), multiple disabilities, physical disabilities, and speech and language. In addition, books for six chronic illnesses are included: AIDS, allergies, asthma, cancer, diabetes, and epilepsy. See Chapter 6 for annotated bibliographies.

Books Listed by Disability or Chronic Illness

Autism or Autistic-like Behavior:
Amenta, Charles A. *Russell is Extra Special: A Book About Autism for Children.*

Blindness, Low Vision or Partially Sighted:
Alexander, Sally Hobart. *Mom Can't See Me.*

Alexander, Sally Hobart. *Mom's Best Friend.*

Allen, Anne. *Sports for the Handicapped.*

Arnold, Caroline. *A Guide Dog Puppy Grows Up.*

Barrett, Mary Brigid. *Sing To The Stars.*

Brown, Tricia. *Someone Special, Just Like You.*

Cohen, Miriam. *See You Tomorrow, Charles.*

Condra, Estelle. *See The Ocean.*

Golden, Barbara Diamond. *Cakes and Miracles.*

Greenfield, Eloise. *William and the Good Old Days.*

Karim, Roberta. *Mandy Sue Day.*

Kastner, Jill. *Naomi Knows It's Springtime.*

MacLachlan, Patricia. *Through Grandpa's Eyes.*

Martin, Bill J.R. *Knots on a Counting Rope.*

Moon, Nicola. *Lucy's Pictures.*

Newth, Philip. *Roly Goes Exploring.*

Pearson, Susan. *Happy Birthday, Grampie.*

Sargent, Susan & Wirt, Donna Aaron, *My Favorite Place.*

Simpson-Smith, Elizabeth. *A Guide Dog Goes To School.*

Chronic Illness:

Alden, Joan. *A Boy's Best Friend.* (asthma)

Althea. *I Have Diabetes.* (diabetes)

Amadeo, Diane M. *There's A Little Bit Of Me In Jamey.* (cancer)

Calmenson, Stephanie. *Rosie: A Visiting Dog's Story.* (variety)

Coerr, Eleanor. *Sadako.* (leukemia)

Delton, Judy. *I'll Never Love Anything Ever Again.* (allergies)

Gaes, Jason. *My Book For Kids With Cansur.* (cancer)

Girard, Linda W. Alex, *The Kid With AIDS.* (AIDS)

Jordon, MaryKate. *Losing Uncle Tim.* (AIDS)

Kornfield, Elizabeth J. *Dreams Come True.* (epilepsy)

Krisher, Trudy. *Kathy's Hats: A Story of Hope.* (cancer)

London, Jonathan. *The Lion Who Has Asthma.* (asthma)

Merrifield, Margaret. *Come Sit By Me.* (AIDS)

Montoussamy-Ashe, Jeanne. *Daddy & Me.* (AIDS)

Moss, Deborah M. *Lee, the Rabbit with Epilepsy.* (epilepsy)

Pirner, Connie White. *Even Little Kids Get Diabetes*. (diabetes).

Porte, Barbara Ann. *Harry's Dog*. (allergies)

Quinlan, Patricia. *Tiger Flowers*. (AIDS)

Rogers, Alison. *Luke Has Asthma*. (asthma)

Rosenberg, Maxine B. *Finding A Way: Living with Exceptional Brothers and Sisters*. (diabetes and asthma)

Silverstein, A. Ivin, & Silverstein, Virginia B. *Runaway Sugar: All About Diabetes*. (diabetes)

Swanson, Susanne M. *My Friend Emily*. (epilepsy)

Verniero, Joan C. *You Can Call Me Willy*. (HIV - AIDS)

Weiner, Lori S., Best, Aprille, & Pizzo, Philip A. *Be A Friend*. (HIV)

Deafness or Hearing Impaired:
Allen, Anne. *Sports for the Handicapped*.

Ancona, George and Ancona, Mary Beth. *Handtalk Zoo*.

Bergman, Thomas. *Going Places: Children Living with Cerebral Palsy*.

Booth, Barbara. *Mandy*.

Brown, Tricia. *Someone Special, Just Like You*.

Chaplin, Susan Gibbons. *I Can Sign My ABCs*.

Charlip, Remy. *Handtalk Birthday*.

Greenberg, Judith E. *What Is the Sign for Friend?*

Hesse, Karen. *Lester's Dog*.

Lakin, Patricia. *Dad and Me In The Morning*.

Lee, Jeanne M. *Silent Lotus*.

Levi, Dorothy Hoffman. *A Very Special Friend*.

Levi, Dorothy Hoffman. *A Very Special Sister*.

Levine, Edna S. *Lisa and Her Soundless World*.

Litchfield, Ada B. *A Button In Her Ear.*

Litchfield, Ada B. *Words in Our Hands.*

Peterson, Jeanne Whitehouse. *I Have A Sister My Sister Is Deaf.*

Rankin, Laura. *The Handmade Alphabet.*

Sanford, Doris. *David Has AIDS.*

Slier, Debby. *Animal Signs: A First Book of Sign Language.*

Slier, Debby. *Word Signs: A First Book of Sign Language.*

Wahl, Jan. *Jamie's Tiger.*

Zelonski, Joy. *I Can't Always Hear You.*

Emotional and Behavioral Disorders:
Loski, Diana. *The Boy on The Bus.* (ADD)

Moss, Deborah M. *Shelley The Hyperactive Turtle.* (ADHD)

Gehret, Jeanne. *Eagle Eyes.* (ADD)

Learning Disability:
Cohen, Miriam. *It's George.*

Dwyer, Kathleen M. *What Do You Mean I Have A Learning Disability?*

O'Shaughnessy, Ellen. *Somebody Called Me A Retard Today…and My Heart Felt Sad.*

Sanford, Doris. *Don't Look At Me.*

Mental Retardation:
Allen, Anne. *Sports for the Handicapped.*

Bergman, Thomas. *We Laugh, We Love, We Cry: Children Living with Mental Retardation.*

Brown, Tricia. *Someone Special, Just Like You.*

Bunnett, Rochelle. *Friends in The Park.*

Cairo, Shelley. *Our Brother Has Down's Syndrome.*

Cohen, M. *It's George.*

Dwight, Laura. *We Can Do It!*

Haines, Sandra. *Becca and Sue Make Two.*

Litchfield, Ada B. *Making Room for Uncle Joe.*

O'Shaughnessy, Ellen. *Somebody Called Me A Retard Today...and My Heart Felt Sad.*

Rabe, Berniece. *Where's Chimpy?*

Sanford, Doris. *Don't Look At Me.*

Wright, Betty Ren. *My Sister Is Different.*

Multiple Disabilities:
Emmert, Michelle. *I'm The Big Sister Now.*

Moran, George. *Imagine Me on a Sit-Ski!*

Rosenberg, Maxine B. *My Friend Leslie: The Story of a Handicapped Child.*

Thompson, Mary. *My Brother Matthew.*

Physical Disability:
Allen, Anne. *Sports for the Handicapped.*

Bergman, Thomas. *Going Places: Children Living with Cerebral Palsy.*

Brown, Tricia. *Someone Special, Just Like You.*

Bunnett, Rochelle. *Friends in The Park.*

Bunting, Eve. *The Sunshine Home.*

Bunting, Eve. *The Wall.*

Calmenson, Stephanie. *Rosie: A Visiting Dog's Story.*

Carlson, Nancy. *Arnie and the New Kid.*

Caseley, Judith. *Apple Pie and Onions.*

Caseley, Judith. *Harry and Willy and Carrothead.* (prosthesis)

Cowen-Fletcher, Jane. *Mama Zooms.*

Damrell, Liz. *With The Wind.*

Dwight, Laura. *We Can Do It!* (spina bifida)

Edwards, Michelle. *alef-bet – A Hebrew Alphabet Book.*

Greenfield, Eloise. *William and the Good Old Days.*

Haldane, Suzanne. *Helping Hands: How Monkeys Assist People Who Are Disabled.* (quadriplegia)

Hamm, Diane Johnson. *Grandma Drives a Motor Bed.*

Hearn, Emily. *Franny and the Music Girl.*

Hearn, Emily. *Good Morning Franny, Good Night Franny.*

Henriod, Lorraine. *Grandma's Wheelchair.*

Hines, Anna Grossnickle. *Gramma's Walk.*

Holcomb, Nan. *Fair and Square.* (switches)

Holcomb, Nan. *Patrick and Emma Lou.* (cerebral palsy)

Kuklin, Susan. *Thinking Big: The Story of a Young Dwarf.*

Lasker, Joe. *Nick Joins In.*

Lyon, George Ella. *Cecil's Story.*

Mayer, Gina & Mercer. *A Very Special Critter.*

Moran, George. *Imagine Me on a Sit-Ski!*

Muldoon, Kathleen M. *Princess Pooh.*

Muller, Gerda. *A Garden in The City.*

Osofsky, Audrey. *My Buddy.* (muscular dystrophy)

Peckinpah, Sandra Lee. *Chester…The Imperfect All-Star.* (limb missing)

Powers, Mary Ellen. *Our Teacher's in a Wheelchair.* (paraplegia)

Rabe, Berniece. *The Balancing Girl.*

Raffi. *One Light, One Sun.*

Rosenberg, Maxine B. *Finding A Way: Living with Exceptional Brothers and Sisters.* (spina bifida)

Russo, Marisabina. *Alex is My Friend.* (small in stature)

Sanford, Doris. *Help! Fire!* (limbs missing)

Seuling, Barbara. *I'm Not So Different.*

Taylor, Ron. *All by Self.* (cerebral palsy)

Thompson, Mary. *My Brother Matthew.* (brain damage)

Whinston, Joan Lenett. *I'm Joshua & Yes I Can.* (cerebral palsy)

White, Paul. *Janet at School.*

Wright, Christine. *Just Like Emma: How She Has Fun in God's World.* (spina bifida)

Speech and Language:
Holcomb, Nan. *Sarah's Surprise.*

Moran, George. *Imagine Me on a Sit-Ski!*

Peckinpah, Sandra Lee. *Rosie...The Imperfect Angel.*

Thompson, Mary. *My Brother Matthew.*

Notes

CHAPTER EIGHT

Children's Books Cross-Referenced According to How the Disability Is Treated

Introduction

The books in this bibliography were analyzed to determine how the authors treated or incorporated the information about the disability or illness. This information will be helpful when selecting literature for young children. Three categories were identified:

Category A: Books provide information about disability or illness.
Category B: Books provide stories about disability or illness.
Category C: Provides stories with character(s) with disability or illness

Each category has its place in the disability literature for young children. Books in Category A provide information and are especially effective when you want children to learn about a specific disability or illness. Books in Category B provide information but in a story format which may hold a young child's interest longer, but often the information does not have as much depth as books in Category A. Books in Category C are very important as they allow children to see characters of varying abilities in the storyline. These stories integrate persons with disabilities or illness in a natural way much like what children see in their schools or community. Children with disabilities and illness are able to see people like themselves in the stories they read, and children without disabilities begin to learn about people who are different from themselves.

Books Listed by Category

Category A
Books Provide Information About Disability or Chronic Illness

Alexander, Sally Hobart. *Mom Can't See Me.*

Alexander, Sally Hobart. *Mom's Best Friend.*

Allen, Anne. *Sports for the Handicapped.*

Althea. *I Have Diabetes.*

Amenta, Charles A. *Russell is Extra Special: A Book About Autism for Children.*

Bergman, Thomas. *Going Places: Children Living with Cerebral Palsy.*

Bergman, Thomas. *We Laugh, We Love We Cry: Children Living with Mental Retardation.*

Brown, Tricia. *Someone Special, Just Like You.*

Cairo, Shelley. *Our Brother Has Down's Syndrome.*

Calmenson, Stephanie. *Rosie: A Visiting Dog's Story.*

Chaplin, Susan Gibbons. *I Can Sign My ABCs.*

Dwight, Laura. *We Can Do It.*

Dwyer, Kathleen. *What Do You Mean I Have A Learning Disability?*

Emmert, Michelle. *I'm The Big Sister Now.*

Gaes, Jason. *My Book for Kids with Cansur.*

Haldane, Suzanne. *Helping Hands: How Monkeys Assist People Who Are Disabled.*

Kornfield, Elizabeth J. *Dreams Come True.*

Litchfield. Ada. *Words in Our Hands.*

Levine, Edna S. *Lisa And Her Soundless World.*

Montoussamy-Ashe, Jeanne. *Daddy & Me.*

O'Shaughnessy, Ellen. *Somebody Called Me a Retard Today…and My Heart Felt Sad.*

Osofsky, Audrey. *My Buddy.*

Peterson, Jeanne. *I Have A Sister My Sister is Deaf.*

Pirner, Connie White. *Even Little Kids Get Diabetes.*

Powers, Mary Ellen. *Our Teacher's in a Wheelchair.*

Rankin, Laura. *The Handmade Alphabet.*

Rosenberg, Maxine B. *Finding A Way: Living with Exceptional Brothers and Sisters.*

Sanford, Doris. *Don't Look At Me.*

Silverstein, Alvin & Silverstein, Virginia. *Runaway Sugar*.

Simpson-Smith, Elizabeth. *A Guide Dog Goes to School*.

Slier, Debby. *Animal Signs: A First Book of Sign Language*.

Slier, Debby. *Word Signs: A First Book of Signs*.

Taylor, Ron. *All By Self*.

White, Paul. *Janet at School*.

Wiener, Lori, Best, Aprille, & Pizzo, Philip. *Be A Friend*.

Category B
Stories About Disability or Chronic Illness

Amadeo, Diane M. *There's A Little Bit Of Me In Jamey*.

Ancona, George, & Ancona, Mary Beth. *Handtalk Zoo*.

Arnold, Caroline. *A Guide Dog Puppy Grows Up*.

Bunnett, Rochelle. *Friends in the Park*.

Bunting, Eve. *The Sunshine Home*.

Carlson, Nancy. *Arnie And The New Kid*.

Caseley, Judith. *Harry and Willy and Carrothead*.

Charlip, Remy. *Handtalk Birthday*.

Coerr, Eleanor. *Sadako*.

Cohen, Miriam. *It's George*.

Cohen, Miriam. *See You Tomorrow, Charles*.

Cowen-Fletcher, Jane. *MaMa Zooms*.

Delton, Judy. *I'll Never Love Anything Ever Again*.

Gehret, Jeanne. *Eagle Eyes*.

Girard, Linda W. *Alex, the Kid with AIDS*.

Golden, Barbara Diamond. *Cakes and Miracles*.

Haines, Sandra. *Becca and Sue Make Two*.

Hamm, Diane Johnston. *Grandma Drives a Motor Bed.*

Holcomb, Nan. *Fair and Square.*

Holcomb, Nan. *Patrick and Emma Lou.*

Holcomb, Nan. *Sarah's Surprise.*

Jordon, MaryKate. *Losing Uncle Tim.*

Krisher, Trudy. *Kathy's Hats: A Story of Hope.*

Kuklin, Susan. *Thinking Big.*

Lasker, Joe. *Nick Joins In.*

Lee, Jeanne M. *Silent Lotus.*

Levi, Dorothy Hoffman. *A Very Special Friend.*

Levi, Dorothy Hoffman. *A Very Special Sister.*

Litchfield, Ada. *A Button In Her Ear.*

Litchfield, Ada. *Making Room for Uncle Joe.*

London, Jonathan. *The Lion Who Has Asthma.*

Loski, Diana. *The Boy on The Bus.*

MacLachlan, Patricia. *Through Grandpa's Eyes.*

Martin, Bill J.R. *Knots on a Counting Rope.*

Mayer, Bina & Mercer. *A Very Special Critter.*

Merrifield, Margaret. *Come Sit By Me.*

Moran, George. *Imagine Me on a Sit-Ski!*

Moss, Deborah. *Lee, The Rabbit with Epilepsy.*

Moss, Deborah. *Shelley, The Hyperactive Turtle.*

Muldoon, Kathleen M. *Princess Pooh.*

Peckinpah, Sandra Lee. *Chester…The Imperfect All-Star.*

Peckinpah, Sandra Lee. *Rosie…The Imperfect Angel.*

Porte, Barbara Ann. *Harry's Dog.*

Quinlan, Patricia. *Tiger Flowers.*

Rogers, Alison. *Luke Has Asthma, Too.*

Rosenberg, Maxine B. *My Friend Leslie: The Story of a Handicapped Child.*

Russo, Marisabina. *Alex is My Friend.*

Sanford, Doris. *David Has AIDS.*

Sanford, Doris. *Help! Fire!*

Seuling, Barbara. *I'm Not So Different.*

Swanson, Susanne M. *My Friend Emily.*

Thompson, Mary. *My Brother Matthew.*

Verniero, Joan. *You Can Call Me Willy.*

Wahl, Jan. *Jamie's Tiger.*

Whinston, Joan Lenett. *I'm Joshua and "Yes I Can".*

Wright, Betty Ren. *My Sister is Different.*

Wright, Christine. *Just Like Emma.*

Zelonski, Joy. *I Can't Always Hear You.*

Category C
Stories With Character(s) With Disability or Chronic Illness

Alden, Joan. *A Boy's Best Friend.*

Barrett, Mary Brigid. *Sing to The Stars.*

Booth, Barbara. *Mandy.*

Bunting, Eve. *The Wall.*

Caseley, Judith. *Apple Pie and Onions.*

Condra, Estelle. *See The Ocean.*

Damrell, Liz. *With The Wind.*

Edwards, Michelle. *alef-bet – A Hebrew Alphabet Book.*

Greenfield, Eloise. *William and the Good Old Days*.

Hearn, Emily. *Franny and the Music Girl*.

Hearn, Emily. *Good Morning Franny, Good Night Franny*.

Henriod, Lorraine. *Grandma's Wheelchair*.

Hesse, Karen. *Lester's Dog*.

Hines, Anna Grossnickle. *Gramma's Walk*.

Karim, Roberta. *Mandy Sue Day*.

Kastner, Jill. *Naomi Knows It's Springtime*.

Lakin, Patricia. *Dad and Me in the Morning*.

Lyon, George Ella. *Cecil's Story*.

Moon, Nicola. *Lucy's Pictures*.

Muller, Gerda. *The Garden in The City*.

Newth, Philip. *Roly Goes Exploring*.

Pearson, Susan. *Happy Birthday, Grampie*.

Rabe, Berniece. *The Balancing Girl*.

Rabe, Berniece. *Where's Chimpy?*

Raffi. *One Light, One Sun*.

Sargent, Susan, & Wirt, Donna Aaron. *My Favorite Place*.

CHAPTER NINE

Using the Theme Approach: Children's Books Cross-Referenced by Theme

Introduction

Most early childhood professionals use a theme or literacy-based approach to their teaching and need children's books that relate to their chosen theme. Often parents seek books with a particular theme. To assist in the selection of literature by theme, the books have been analyzed to identify the theme or themes into which the books can be appropriately incorporated. In this bibliography, the books are listed by theme with 4 themes represented. Many of the books relate to more than one theme so are listed multiple times.

Using the Theme Approach

Many early childhood professionals teach or work with children using a theme approach in their curriculum planning. The professional selects an idea or concept and plans all of the activities for the day or several days around this concept. For example, a unit using the theme of Shapes might plan the snack to be different shaped crackers and cheese cut into shapes; the art center might have various shapes of sponges for painting; gross motor activities might have the children walking, crawling, and hopping on lines made into common shapes. The quiet center would have books about shapes available for the children's choosing. The concept of shapes would be incorporated into every activity in the unit. The books selected to be used in this theme on Shapes, should represent people of diversity which includes persons of diverse abilities (i.e. disability and illness).

A theme analysis has been conducted on the books in this bibliography to determine into which theme(s) the books can be incorporated. Through this analysis, books were identified that could be used in 49 different themes. Using the Theme Bibliography, parents and professionals can quickly identify books that can be easily incorporated into a variety of themes or units.

Developing Text Sets

A Text Set is two or more books that are related in some way. The relationship between the books might be by theme, topic, author, text organization or any other relationship that can be identified. The reason for grouping books is because books read and considered together are much more powerful than when each is considered alone (Heine, 1991).

Text Sets foster critical thinking as readers look for relationships. They are used to facilitate discussion and learning as the readers make connections between stories and their own personal stories (Heine, 1991). This process can occur with children as young as those in early childhood programs. Consider a Text Set of books about families. One book is about an African-American family, one is about a Caucasian dad raising a child alone, and the third is about a family who has a child with a disability. By reading all three books in this Set, children are able to make relationships and learn more about families than by merely reading any one of the books. This demonstrates the power of grouping books into Text Sets.

For discussion purposes, it is best to limit the number of books in the Text Set to three or four (Harste, Short, & Burke, 1988). In early childhood programs it may be necessary to limit Sets to only two or three books. While two or three books may be the focus of discussion, there may be a larger Text Set from which teachers and children select the books for discussion. An example of a small Text Set on transportation for preschoolers might include the following books:

> *This Is The Way We Go To School* – Baer
> *All Aboard ABC* – Magee & Newman
> *Zoomrimes: Poems About Things That Go* – Cassedy
> *Mama Zooms* – Cowen-Fletcher
> *Here Come The Monster Trucks* – Sullivan
> *Inside A Freight Train* – McHenry

In this Text Set, *This Is The Way We Go To School* incorporates cultural diversity, while *Mama Zooms* incorporates diversity of ability.

Most of the Text Sets used in early childhood programs tend to be related by theme. One of the problems is that books portraying persons with disabilities are rarely included. Surveys of teachers have indicated that they often lack familiarity with the disability literature and do not know which books are available and would be appropriate to include. The Theme Bibliography provides a list of books which can easily be incorporated into Text Sets related by theme. The Text Set Lesson Plans in Chapter 10 provide a format for you to develop your own Lesson Plans by simply adding book titles. The disability literature is listed for you.

Literature-Based Approach

Many early childhood professionals use a literature-based approach to develop their curriculum. This means that one main story is selected around which all of the activities for that day or several days relate in some way. For example, the main book selection might be *Corduroy*. This is an adventure of a teddy bear who searches for his missing button and finds a friend. All of the curricular activities will relate in some way to this story. For example, the children might act out parts of the story. Snack might be foods that bears eat. Gross motor might be the activity "Going on a Bear Hunt." The professional can stress any concept that is represented in the story such as friendship. If friendship is the concept being stressed, additional books about friendship would be available. The Theme Bibliography has the theme of Friendship listed with a number of books identified that stress friendship while including a character in the story who has a disability or chronic illness. For example, *Come Sit By Me*, is a delightful story about a friendship at school with a child who has AIDS. In addition to the concept of friendship, the children also have the opportunity to learn something about the disability or illness represented in the book. It becomes a time for them to ask questions and learn. Integrating learning about disabilities or illnesses throughout the curriculum is a natural way for children to learn. This makes more sense to young children than by learning about disabilities only during "Disability Awareness Week."

When books are selected for each theme, it's important that some selections incorporate diversity of culture and ability. It seems that efforts to increase the use of multicultural literature with young children has steadily progressed over recent years, while the use of literature about disabilities and illness has been left far behind. The Theme Bibliography will provide you with books that can be easily selected for inclusion into your units and can represent diversity of ability.

Books Cross-Referenced by Theme

When using the Theme Bibliography, look up the theme that is of interest to you. If that theme is not on the list, look up a related theme. For example if you want to read a book about monkeys or are teaching a unit on monkeys, you would look up the theme "Monkeys." You would find that there is no theme exclusively about monkeys. Next, you would look for a related theme. In this search you would find that there is a theme or unit on "Zoo Animals." This is where you would look to find an appropriate book for your unit or your reading pleasure. Under "Zoo Animals" you would find three books about monkeys that could be used. There will be times when you will be unable to find books related to a particular theme. This is because the collection of literature for young children that includes a character with a disability is limited. However, additional books are being written each year that you will want to add to your lesson plans.

Apples
Caseley, J. *Apple Pie and Onions*, Gr. K-3. Disability: Physical. (****)

Beach Party or Seashore
Hines, A. G. *Gramma's Walk*, Gr. PS-2. Disability: Physical. (****)

Raffi. *One Light, One Sun*, Gr. PS-2. Disability: Physical. (****)

Sargent, S. & Wirt, D. A. *My Favorite Place*, Gr. PS-3. Disability: Blind. (***)

Body Awareness
Badt, K.L. *Hair There and Everywhere*, Gr. 1-5. Differences. (****)

Homanako, S. *All The Colors of the Earth*, Gr. PS-3. Differences. (****)

Nikola-Lisa, W. *Bein' With You This Way*, Gr. PS-3. Differences. (****)

Quinsey, M. B. *Why Does That Man Have Such A Big Nose?* Gr. PS-3. Differences. (****)

Russo, M. *Alex is My Friend*, Gr. PS-2. Disability: Physical (size). (****)

Spier, P. *People*, Gr. All Ages. Differences. (****)

Brothers & Sisters
Amadeo, D. *There's A Little Bit Of Me In Jamey*, Gr. 1-4. Illness: Cancer. (****)

Cairo, S. *Our Brother Has Down's Syndrome*, Gr. K-3. Disability: Down Syndrome. (****)

de Poix, C. *Jo, Flo, and Yolanda*, Gr. PS-3. Differences. (****)

Emmert, M. *I'm The Big Sister Now*, Gr. K-3. Disability: Cerebral Palsy, Severe Brain Damage (multiple Disabilities). (****)

Gehret, J. Eagle Eyes, Gr. 1-5. *Disability/Illness: Attention Deficit Disorder.* (****)

Levi, D.H. *A Very Special Sister*, Gr. PS-2. Disability: Deafness. (****)

Muldoon, K. M. *Princess Pooh*, Gr. 2-5. Disability: Physical. (****)

Peterson, J. W. *I Have A Sister My Sister Is Deaf*, Gr. PS-3. Disability: Deaf. (***)

Rosenberg, M. D. *Finding A Way: Living with Exceptional Brothers and Sisters*, Gr. K-3. Disability/Illness: Diabetes, Asthma, Spina Bifida. (****)

Thompson, M. *My Brother Matthew*, Gr. K-3. Disability: Physical and Speech/Language Delay. (****)

Wright, B.R. *My Sister is Different*, Gr. K-3. Disability: Mental Retardation. (****)

Wright, C. *Just Like Emma: How She Has Fun in God's World*, Gr. K-3. Disability: Physical. (****)

Buildings
Dorros, A. *This is My House*, Gr. PS-2. Differences. (****)

Lasker, J. *Nick Joins In*, Gr. 2-3. Disability: Physical. (***)

Raffi. *One Light, One Sun*, Gr. PS-2. Disability: Physical. (****)

Spier, P. *People*, Gr. All Ages, Differences. (****)

Children and Families Around the World

Badt, K.L. *Hair There and Everywhere*, Gr. 1-5. Differences. (****)

Baer, E. *This is the Way We Go to School*, Gr. PS-3. Differences.

Dorros, A. *This is My House*, Gr. PS-2. Differences. (****)

Edwards, M. *alef-bet - A Hebrew Alphabet Book*, Gr. K-2. Disability: Physical. (****)

Golden, B. D. *Cakes and Miracles*, Gr. K-4. Disability: Blindness. (****)

Hamanaka, S. *All The Colors of The Earth*, Gr. PS-3. Differences. (****)

Hearn, E. *Good Morning Franny, Good Night Franny*, Gr. PS-3. Disability: Physical. (****)

Leventhal, D. *What Is Your Language?* Gr. PS-3. Differences. (****)

Martin, Bill J. R. *Knots on a Counting Rope*, Gr. K-3. Disability: Blind. (****)

Morris, A. *Hats Hats Hats*, Gr. PS-2. Differences. (****)

Pearson, S. *Happy Birthday, Grampie*, Gr. PS-3. Disability: Blindness. (****)

Simon, N. *All Kinds of Families*, Gr. PS-3. Differences. (****)

Spier, P. *People*, Gr. All Ages. Differences. (****)

Circus, Circus Animals, Clowns

Haldane, S. *Helping Hands: How Monkeys Assist People Who are Disabled*, Gr. 3-7. Disability: Physical. (****) (monkey)

Rabe, B. *Where's Chimpy?* Gr. K-3. Disability: Physical. (****) (monkey)

City

Barrett, M.B. *Sing To The Stars*, Gr. PS-3. Disability: Blindness. (****)

Hearn, E. *Good Morning Franny, Good Night Franny*, Gr. PS-3. Disability: Physical. (****)

Hearn, E. *Franny and The Music Girl*, Gr. PS-2. Disability: Physical. (****)

Takeshita, F. *The Park Bench*, Gr. K-2. Differences. (****)

Colors in My World

Holy Cross Kindergartners, *What's Under Your Hood, Orson?* Gr. PS-1 Differences. (****) (red, yellow, blue)

Hamanako, S. *All The Colors of the Earth*, Gr. PS-3. Differences. (****) (many)

Merrifield, M. *Come Sit By Me*, Gr. PS-3. Illness: HIV - AIDS. (****) (many)

Moon, N. *Lucy's Pictures*, Gr. PS-3. Disability: Blindness. (****) (many)

Rabe, B. *The Balancing Girl*, Gr. PS-2. Disability: Physical. (****) (red)

Raffi. *One Light, One Sun*, Gr. PS-2. Disability: Physical. (****) (yellow).

Community Workers

Powers, M. E. *Our Teacher's in a Wheelchair*, Gr. PS-3. Disability: Physical. (****) (teacher)

Sanford, S. *Help! Fire!* Gr. K-3. Disability: Physical. (****) (Firepeople)

Takeshita, F. *The Park Bench*, Gr. K-2. Differences. (****) (Park Worker)

Day and Night

Booth, B. *Mandy*, Gr. PS-2. Disability: Deafness. (****)

Lakin, P. *Dad and Me in the Morning*, Gr. PS-2. Disability: Deafness. (****)

Raffi. *One Light, One Sun*, Gr. PS-2. Disability: Physical. (****)

Dentist, Doctors, Nurses and Hospitals

Amadeo, D. M. *There's A Little Bit Of Me In Jamey*, Gr. 1-4. Cancer. (****)

Bunting, E. *The Sunshine Home*, Gr. K-3. Nursing Home. Disability: Physical. (****)

Gaes, J. *My Book For Kids With Cansur*, Gr. PS-4. Illness: Cancer. (****)

Hamm, D. J. *Grandma Drives a Motor Bed*, Gr. 1-3. Disability: Physical. (****)

Litchfield, A. B. *A Button In Her Ear*, Gr. K-3. Disability: Hearing Loss. (****)

Macdonald, M. *Little Hippo Gets Glasses*, Gr. PS-3. Differences. (****)

Moss, D. M. *Lee, the Rabbit with Epilepsy*, Gr. K-4. Disability: Epilepsy. (***)

Moss. D. M. *Shelley The Hyperactive Turtle*, Gr. K-3. Hyperactivity. (**)

Pearson, S. *Happy Birthday, Grampie*, Gr. PS-3. Disability: Blindness. (****)

Pirner, C. W. *Even Little Kids Get Diabetes*, Gr. PS-2. Illness: Diabetes. (****)

Families

Alden, J. *A Boy's Best Friend*, Gr. PS-2. Illness: Asthma. (****)

Alexander, S H. *Mom Can't See Me*, Gr. K-3. Disability: Blindness. (****)

Amenta, C. A. *Russell is Extra Special: A Book About Autism for Children*, Gr. PS-2. Disability: Autism. (****)

Bunting, E. *The Sunshine Home*, Gr. K-3. Disability: Physical. (****)

Bunting, E. *The Wall*, Gr. PS-3. Disability: Physical. (****)

Cairo, S. *Our Brother Has Down's Syndrome*, Gr. K-3. Disability: Down Syndrome. (***)

Cheltenham Elem. School. *We Are Alike...We Are All Different*, Gr. PS-2. (****)

Condra, E. *See The Ocean*, Gr. K-3. Disability: Blindness. (****)

Cowen-Fletcher, J. *Mama Zooms*, Gr. PS-2. Disability: Physical. (****)

de Poix, C. *Jo, Flo and Yolanda*, Gr. PS-3. Differences. (****)

Edwards, M. *alef-bet – A Hebrew Alphabet Book*, Gr. K-2. (****)

Emmert, M. *I'm The Big Sister Now*, Gr. K-3. Disability: Cerebral Palsy, Severe Brain Damage (multiple disabilities). (****)

Gehret, J. *Eagle Eyes*, Gr. 1-5. Disability/Illness: Attention Deficit Disorder. (****)

Henriod, L. *Grandma's Wheelchair*, Gr. PS-2. Disability: Physical. (****)

Karim, R. *Mandy Sue Day*, Gr. PS-3. Disability: Blindness. (****)

Lakin, P. *Dad and Me in the Morning*, Gr. PS-2. Disability: Deafness. (****)

Litchfield, A. B. *Making Room for Uncle Joe*, Gr. 1-4. Disability: Down Syndrome. (***)

Litchfield, A.B. *Words In Our Hands*, Gr. K-3. Disability: Deafness. (***)

Lyon, G. *Cecil's Story*, Gr. K-3. Disability: Physical (lost limb). (****)

MacLachlan, P. *Through Grandpa's Eyes*, Gr. K-3. Disability: Blindness. (****)

Martin, Bill J. R. *Knots on a Counting Rope*, Gr. K-3. Disability: Blindness. (****)

Montoussamy-Ashe, J. *Daddy & Me*, Gr. PS-3. Chronic Illness: AIDS. (****)

Moss, D. M. *Lee, the Rabbit with Epilepsy*, Gr. K-4. Disability: Epilepsy. (***)

Pearson, S. *Happy Birthday, Grampie*, Gr. PS-3. Disability: Blindness. (****)

Peterson, J. W. *I Have A Sister My Sister Is Deaf*, Gr. PS-3. Disability: Deafness. (****)

Quinlan, P. *Tiger Flowers*, Gr. K-3. Illness: AIDS. (****)

Rabe, B. *Where's Chimpy?* Gr. PS-2. Disability: Down Syndrome. (****)

Raffi. *One Light, One Sun*, Gr. PS-2. Disability: Physical (wheelchair). (****)

Rosenberg, M. B. *Finding A Way: Living with Exceptional Brothers and Sisters*, Gr. K-3. Disability/Illness: Diabetes, Asthma, & Spina Bifida. (****)

Seuling, B. *I'm Not So Different*, Gr. K-3. Disability: Physical (wheelchair). (****)

Simon, N. *All Kinds of Families*, Gr. PS-3. Differences. (****)

Simon, N. *Why Am I Different?* Gr. PS-3. Differences. (****)

Taylor, R. *All By Self*, Gr. K-6. Disability: Cerebral Palsy (wheelchair). (****)

Thompson, M. *My Brother Matthew*, Gr. K-3. Disability: Physical, Speech/Language Delay (brain injury). (****)

White, P. *Janet at School*, Gr. PS-2. Disability: Physical, Spina Bifida (leg braces & wheelchair). (***)

Wright, C. *Just Like Emma: How She Has Fun in God's World*, Gr. K-3. Disability: Physical (spina bifida). (****)

Families at Work
Alexander, S. H. *Mom Can't See Me*, Gr. K-3. Disability: Blindness. (****) (Occupation – writer)

Farm and Farm Animals
Damrell, L. *With The Wind*, Gr. PS-2. Disability: Physical. (****) (horses)

Karim, R. *Mandy Sue Day*, Gr. PS-3. Disability: Blindness. (****) (horse)

Slier, D. *Animal Signs: A First Book of Sign Language*, Gr. PS-K. Disability: Hearing Loss, Deafness (signing). (****)

Feelings

Amadeo, D.M. *There's A Little Bit Of Me In Jamey*, Gr. 1-4. Chronic Illness: Cancer. (****)

Baer, E. *This is the Way We Go to School*, Gr. PS-3. Differences. (****)

Brown, M. *Arthur's Eyes*, Gr. PS-3. Differences. (***)

Bunting, E. *The Sunshine Home*, Gr. K-3. Disability: Physical. (****)

Bunting, E. *The Wall*, Gr. PS-3. Disability: Physical. (****)

Carlson, N. *Arnie and the New Kid*, Gr. PS-3. Disability: Physical (wheelchair). (****)

Caseley, J. *Apple Pie and Onions*, Gr. K-3. Disability: Physical (wheelchair). (****)

Caseley, J. *Harry and Willy and Carrothead*, Gr. K-3. Disability: Physical (prosthesis for left hand). (****)

Damrell, L. *With The Wind*, Gr. PS-2. Disability: Physical (leg braces & wheelchair). (****)

Delton, J. *I'll Never Love Anything Ever Again*, Gr. PS-3. Chronic Illness: Allergies. (****)

Dwyer, K. *What Do You Mean I Have A Learning Disability?* Gr. 1-5. Disability: Learning Disability. (***)

Gehret, J. *Eagle Eyes*, Gr. 1-5. Disability/Illness: Attention Deficit Disorder (ADD). (****)

Hesse, K. *Lester's Dog*, Gr. PS-3. Disability: Deafness. (****)

Jordon, M. *Losing Uncle Tim*, Gr. K-3. Chronic Illness: AIDS. (****)

Krisher, T. *Kathy's Hats: A Story of Hope*, Gr. PS-2. Chronic Illness: Cancer. (****)

Lasker, J. *Nick Joins In*, Gr. 2-3. Disability: Physical. (***)

Lee, J.M. *Silent Lotus*, Gr. K-3. Disability: Deafness. (****)

Levi, D. H. *A Very Special Friend*, Gr. K-3. Disability: Deafness. (****)

Litchfield, A. B. *Making Room for Uncle Joe*, Gr. 1-4. Disability: Down Syndrome. (***)

Loski, D. *The Boy On The Bus*, Gr. 1-3. Illness: Attention Deficit Disorder ADD). (****)

Lyon, G. *Cecil's Story*, Gr. K-3. Disability: Physical (limb missing). (****)

Macdonald, M. *Little Hippo Gets His Glasses*, Gr. PS-3. Differences. (****)

McDonald, M. *The Potato Man*, Gr. PS-2. Differences. (****)

Muldoon, K. M. *Princess Pooh*, Gr. 2-5. Disability: Physical (crutches, wheelchair). (****)

O'Shaughnessy, E. *Somebody Called Me A Retard Today…and My Heart Felt Sad*, Gr. PS-K. Disability: Mental Retardation, Learning Disability. (****)

Pearson, S. *Happy Birthday, Grampie*, Gr. PS-3. Disability: Blindness. (****)

Peckinpah, S.L. *Rosey: The Imperfect Angel*, Gr. 1-3. Disability: Speech and Language (cleft lip). (***)

Powers, M. E. *Our Teacher's in a Wheelchair*, Gr. PS-3. Disability: Physical (wheelchair). (****)

Quincy, M.B. *Why Does That Man Have Such A Big Nose?* Gr. PS-3. Differences. (****)

Sanford, D. *Don't Look At Me*, Gr. 1-3. Disability: Mental Retardation or Learning Disability. (****)

Simon, N. *Why Am I Different?* Gr. PS-3. Differences. (****)

Taylor, R. *All By Self*, Gr. K-6. Disability: Cerebral Palsy (wheelchair). (****)

Thompson, M. *My Brother Matthew*, Gr. K-3. Disability: Physical and Speech/Language Delay (brain injury). (****)

Verniero, J. *You Can Call Me Willy*, Gr. 1-4. Illness: HIV. (****)

Whinston, J. L. *I'm Joshua & Yes I Can*, Gr. 3-6. Disability: Cerebral Palsy (leg braces). (****)

Wiener, Best, & Pizzo. *Be A Friend*, Gr. All Ages. Illness: HIV – AIDS. (****)

Fish, Fishing
Moss, D. M. *Lee, the Rabbit with Epilepsy*, Gr. K-4. Disability: Epilepsy. (***)

Friends and School
Baer, E. *This is the Way We Go to School*, Gr. PS-3. Differences. (****)

Brown, T. *Someone Special, Just Like You*, Gr. PS-2. Disability: Hearing, Vision, Physical, Down Syndrome. (****)

Carlson, N. *Arnie and the New Kid*, Gr. PS-3. Disability: Physical (wheelchair). (****)

Caseley, J. *Harry and Willy and Carrothead*, Gr. K-3. Disability: Physical (prosthesis for left hand). (****)

Cheltenham Elem. School. *We Are Alike...We Are All Different*, Gr. PS-2. (****)

Cohen, M. *It's George*, Gr. PS-3. Disability: Slow Learner. (***)

Cohen, M. *See You Tomorrow, Charles*, Gr. PS-2. Disability: Blindness. (***)

Dwight, L. *We Can Do It!* Gr. PS-2. Disability: Spina Bifida, Down Syndrome, Cerebral Palsy, Blindness. (****)

Girard, L.W. *Alex, The Kid With AIDS*, Gr. 1-4. Illness: AIDS. (***)

Krisher, T. *Kathy's Hats: A Story of Hope*, Gr. PS-2. Chronic Illness: Cancer. (****)

Lasker, J. *Nick Joins In*, Gr. 2-3. Disability: Physical. (***)

Litchfield, A. B. *A Button In Her Ear*, Gr. K-3. Disability: Hearing Loss. (****)

Loski, D. *The Boy On The Bus*, Gr. 1-3. Disability: ADD. (****)

Macdonald, M. *Little Hippo Gets His Glasses*, Gr. PS-3. Differences. (****)

Mayer, G. & M. *A Very Special Critter*, Gr. PS-3. Disability: Physical. (****)

Merrifield, M. *Come Sit By Me*, Gr. PS-3. Chronic Illness: HIV – AIDS. (****)

Rabe, B. *The Balancing Girl*, Gr. K-3. Disability: Physical. (****)

Rosenberg, M. B. *My Friend Leslie: The Story of a Handicapped Child*, Gr. K-3. Disability: Multiple Disabilities. (****)

Sanford, D. *Don't Look At Me*, Gr. 1-3. Disability: Mental Retardation or Learning Disability. (****)

Verniero, J. *You Can Call Me Willy*, Gr. 1-4. Illness: HIV and AIDS. (****)

Whinston, J. L. *I'm Joshua & Yes I Can*, Gr. 3-6. Disability: Cerebral Palsy. (****)

Zelonski, J. *I Can't Always Hear You*, Gr. K-3. Disability: Deafness. (****)

Friendship

Barrett, M.B. *Sing To The Stars*, Gr. PS-3. Disability: Blindness. (****)

Brown, T. *Someone Special, Just Like You*, Gr. PS-2. Disability: Hearing, Vision, Physical, Down Syndrome. (****)

Bunnett, R. *Friends in The Park*, Gr. PS-1. Disability: Physical, Down Syndrome. (****)

Carlson, N. Arnie and the New Kid, Gr. PS-3. Disability: Physical (wheelchair). (****)

Caseley, J. *Harry and Willy and Carrothead*, Gr. K-3. Disability: Physical (prosthesis for left hand). (****)

Cohen, M. *It's George*, Gr. PS-3. Disability: Slow Learner. (***)

Haines, S. *Becca and Sue Make Two*, Gr. K-3. Disability: Down syndrome. (***)

Hearn, E. *Franny and the Music Girl*, Gr. PS-2. Disability: Physical (wheelchair). (****)

Hearn, E. *Good Morning Franny, Good Night Franny*, Gr. PS-3. Disability: Physical (wheelchair). (****)

Hesse, K. *Lester's Dog*, Gr. PS-3. Disability: Deafness. (****)

Holcomb, N. *Patrick and Emma Lou*, Gr. PS-1. Disability: Physical (cerebral palsy). (***)

Holy Cross Kindergartners. *What's Under Your Hood, Orson?* Gr. PS-1. Differences. (****)

Jordon, M. Losing Uncle Tim, Gr. K-3. Chronic Illness: AIDS. (****)

Lasker, J. *Nick Joins In*, Gr. 2-3. Disability: Physical (leg braces and wheelchair). (***)

Levi, D. H. *A Very Special Friend*, Gr. K-3. Disability: Deafness. (****)

Levi, D.H. *A Very Special Sister*, Gr. K-3. Disability: Deafness. (****)

Macdonald, M. *Little Hippo Gets His Glasses*, Gr. PS-3. Differences. (****)

Merrifield, M. *Come Sit By Me*, Gr. PS-3. Illness: HIV – AIDS. (****)

Nikola-Lisa, W. *Bein' With You This Way*, Gr. PS-3. Differences. (****)

Rabe, B. *The Balancing Girl*, Gr. K-3. Disability: Physical (wheelchair, leg braces, crutches). (****)

Rogers, A. *Luke Has Asthma, Too*, Gr. PS-2. Illness (asthma). (****)

Rosenberg, M. B. *My Friend Leslie: The Story of a Handicapped Child*, Gr. K-3. Disability: Multiple Disabilities. (****)

Russo, M. *Alex is My Friend*, Gr. PS-2. Disability: Physical (growth). (****)

Sanford, D. *David Has AIDS*, Gr. K-2. Illness: AIDS. (****)

Seuling, B. *I'm Not So Different*, Gr. K-3. Disability: Physical (wheelchair). (****)

Simon, N. *Why Am I Different?* Gr. PS-3. Differences. (****)

Swanson, J.S. *My Friend Emily*, Gr. 1-3. Disability/Illness: Epilepsy. (****)

Wahl, J. *Jamie's Tiger*, Gr. PS-3. Disability: Hearing Loss. (****)

Giving and Sharing

Amadeo, D. M. *There's A Little Bit Of Me In Jamey*, Gr. 1-4. Chronic Illness: Cancer. (****)

Arnold, C. *A Guide Dog Puppy Grows Up*, Gr. 1-3. Disability: Blindness. (****)

Calmenson, S. *Rosie: A Visiting Dog's Story*, Gr. PS-3. Disability & Illness. (****)

Carlson, N. *Arnie and the New Kid*, Gr. PS-3. Disability: Physical (wheelchair). (****)

Charlip, R. *Handtalk Birthday*, Gr. K-3. Disability: Deafness. (****)

Hesse, K. *Lester's Dog*, Gr. PS-3. Disability: Deafness. (****)

Litchfield, A. B. *Making Room for Uncle Joe*, Gr. 1-4. Disability: Down Syndrome. (***)

McDonald, M. *The Potato Man*, Gr. PS-2. Differences. (****)

Moon, N. *Lucy's Pictures*, Gr. PS-3. Disability: Blindness. (****)

Pearson, S. *Happy Birthday, Grampie*, Gr. PS-3. Disability: Blindness. (****)

Rogers, A. *Luke Has Asthma, Too*, Gr. PS-2. Illness (asthma). (****)

Russo, M. *Alex is My Friend*, Gr. Ps-2. Disability: Physical (size). (****)

Seuling, B. *I'm Not So Different*, Gr. K-3. Disability: Physical (wheelchair). (****)

Grandmothers and Grandfathers

Amadeo, D. M. *There's A Little Bit Of Me In Jamey*, Gr. 1-4. Chronic Illness: Cancer. (****)

Booth, B. *Mandy*, Gr. PS-2. Disability: Deafness. (****)

Bunting, E. *The Sunshine Home*, Gr. K-3. Disability: Physical. (****)

Caseley, J. *Apple Pie and Onions*, Gr. K-3. Disability: Physical. (****)

Greenfield, E. *William and the Good Old Days*, Fiction, PS-2. Disability: Blindness, Physical (wheelchair). (****)

Hamm, D. J. *Grandma Drives a Motor Bed*, Gr. 1-3. Disability: Physical (wheelchair). (****)

Henriod, L. *Grandma's Wheelchair*, Gr. PS-2. Disability: Physical (wheelchair). (****)

Hines, A. G. *Gramma's Walk*, Gr. PS-2. Disability: Physical (wheelchair). (****)

MacLachlan, P. *Through Grandpa's Eyes*, Gr. K-3. Disability: Blindness. (****)

Martin, Bill J. R. *Knots on a Counting Rope*, K-3. Disability: Blindness. (****)

McDonald, M. *The Potato Man*, Gr. PS-2. Differences. (****)

Moon, N. *Lucy's Pictures*, Gr. PS-3. Disability: Blindness. (****)

Moss, D. M. *Lee, the Rabbit with Epilepsy*, Gr. K-4. Disability: Epilepsy. (***)

Pearson, S. *Happy Birthday, Grampie*, Gr. PS-3. Disability: Blindness. (****)

Simon, N. *All Kinds of Families*, Gr. PS-3. Differences. (****)

Thompson, M. *My Brother Matthew*, Gr. K-3. Disability: Physical, Speech/Language Delay (brain injury). (****)

Hats

Krisher, T. *Kathy's Hats: A Story of Hope*, Gr. PS-2. Chronic Illness: Cancer. (****)

Morris, A. *Hats Hats Hats*, Gr. PS-2. Differences. (****)

Rogers, A. *Luke Has Asthma, Too*, Gr. PS-2. Illness: Asthma. (****)

Spier, P. *People*, Gr. All Ages. Differences. (****)

Health

Alden, J. *A Boy's Best Friend*, Gr. PS-2. Illness: Asthma. (****)

Althea. *I Have Diabetes*, Gr. K-3. Illness: Diabetes. (****)

Amadeo, D. M. *There's A Little Bit Of Me In Jamey*, Gr. 1-4. Illness: Cancer. (****)

Brown, M. *Arthur's Eyes*, Gr. PS-3. Differences. (***)

Bunting, E. *The Sunshine Home*, Gr. K-3. Nursing Home. (****)

Coerr, E. *Sadako*, Gr. 2-6. Illness: Leukemia. (****)

Delton, J. *I'll Never Love Anything Ever Again*, Gr. PS-3. Chronic Illness: Allergies. (****)

Gaes, J. *My Book For Kids With Cansur*, Gr. PS-4. Illness: Cancer. (****)

Gehret, J. *Eagle Eyes*, Gr. 1-5. Disability/Illness: Attention Deficit Disorder. (****)

Girard, L.W. *Alex, The Kid with AIDS*, Gr. 1-4. Illness: AIDS. (***)

Hamm, D. J. *Grandma Drives a Motor Bed*, Gr. 1-3. Disability: Physical (wheelchair). (****)

Jordon, M. *Losing Uncle Tim*, Gr. K-3. Chronic Illness: AIDS. (****)

Kornfield, E. J. *Dreams Come True*, Gr. 1-4. Disability/Chronic Illness: Epilepsy. (****)

Krisher, T. *Kathy's Hats: A Story of Hope*, Gr. PS-2. Illness: Cancer. (****)

London, J. *The Lion Who Has Asthma*, Gr. 1-4. Illness: Asthma. (****)

Macdonald, M. *Little Hippo Gets His Glasses*, Gr. PS-3. Differences. (****)

Merrifield, M. *Come Sit By Me*, Gr. PS-3. Chronic Illness: HIV – AIDS. (****)

Montoussamy-Ashe, J. *Daddy & Me*, Gr. PS-3. Illness: AIDS. (****)

Moss, D. M. *Lee, the Rabbit with Epilepsy*, Gr. K-4. Disability: Epilepsy. (***)

Moss, D. M. *Shelley The Hyperactive Turtle*, Gr. K-3. Disability/Chronic Illness: Hyperactivity. (**)

Pirner, C. W. *Even Little Kids Get Diabetes*, Gr. PS-2. Chronic Illness: Diabetes. (****)

Porte, B. A. *Harry's Dog*, Gr. K-3. Chronic Illness: Allergies. (****)

Quinlin, P. *Tiger Flowers*, Gr. K-3. Illness: AIDS. (****)

Rogers, A. *Luke Has Asthma, Too*, Gr. PS-2. Illness (asthma). (****)

Rosenberg, M. B. *Finding A Way: Living with Exceptional Brothers and Sisters*, Gr. K-3. Disability/Chronic Illness: Diabetes, Asthma, & Spina Bifida. (****)

Sanford, D. *David Has AIDS*, Gr. K-2. Illness: AIDS. (****)

Silverstein, A. I., & Silverstein, V. B. *Runaway Sugar: All About Diabetes*, Gr. 1-3. Chronic Illness: Diabetes. (***)

Swanson, S.M. *My Friend Emily*, Gr. 1-3. Disability/Illness: Epilepsy. (****)

Verniero, J. *You Can Call Me Willy*, Gr. 1-4. Illness: HIV and AIDS. (****)

Wiener, Best, & Pizzo. *Be My Friend*, Gr. All ages. Illness: HIV and AIDS. (****)

Holidays Around the World
Coerr, E. *Sadako*, Gr. 2-6. Illness: Leukemia. (****) (Japanese Memorial Day)

Golden, B. D. *Cakes and Miracles*, Gr. K-4. Disability: Blindness. Holiday: Jewish - Purim. (****)

Holcomb, N. *Sarah's Surprise*, Gr. PS-1. Disability: Speech/Language. (**) (Birthday)

McDonald, M. *The Potato Man*, Gr. PS-2. Differences. (****) (Christmas)

Homes and Neighborhoods
Bunnett, R. *Friends in The Park*, Gr. PS-1. Disability: Physical, Down Syndrome. (****)

Dorros, A. *This is My House*, Gr. PS-2. Differences. (****)

Hearn, E. *Franny and the Music Girl*, Gr. PS-2. Disability: Physical (wheelchair). (****)

Levi, D. H. *A Very Special Friend*, Gr. K-3. Disability: Deafness. (****)

Muller, B. *The Garden in the City*, Gr. 1-4. Disability: Physical. (****)

Nikola-Lisa, W. *Bein' With You This Way*, Gr. PS-3. Differences. (****)

Raffi. *One Light, One Sun*, Gr. PS-2. Disability: Physical (wheelchair). (****)

Simon, N. *Why Am I Different?* Gr. PS-3. Differences. (****)

Spier, P. *People*, Gr. All Ages. Differences. (****)

Naptime and Bedtime
Rabe, B. W*here's Chimpy?*, Gr. PS-2. Disability: Down Syndrome. (****)

Raffi. *One Light, One Sun*, Gr. PS-2. Disability: Physical (wheelchair). (****)

Numbers in My Everyday World
Newth, P. *Roly Goes Exploring*, Gr. PS-2. Disability: Blindness (braille). (***)

Rabe, B. *Where's Chimpy?*, Gr. PS-2. Disability: Down Syndrome. (****)

Oceans, Lakes and Rivers
Condra, E. *See The Ocean*, Gr. K-3. Disability: Blindness. (****)

Lakin, P. *Dad and Me in the Morning*, Gr. K-2. Disability: Deafness. (****)

Sargent, S. & Wirt, D. A. *My Favorite Place*, Gr. PS-3. Disability: Blindness. (***)

Peace Education
Bunting, E. *The Wall*, Gr. PS-3. Disability: Physical. (****)

Coerr, E. *Sadako*, Gr. 2-6. Illness: Leukemia. (****)

Lyon, G. *Cecil's Story*, Gr. K-3. Disability: Physical (limb missing). (****)

Pet Animals/Pet Store
Alden, J. *A Boy's Best Friend*, Gr. PS-2. Illness: Asthma. (****)

Alexander, S. H. *Mom's Best Friend*, Gr. K-3. Disability: Blindness. (****)

Arnold, C. *A Guide Dog Puppy Grows Up*, Gr. 1-3. Disability: Blindness. (****)

Calmenson, S. *Rosie: A Visiting Dog's Story*, Gr. PS-3. Disability and Illness. (****) (dog)

Damrell, L. *With The Wind*, Gr. PS-2. Disability: Physical (leg braces & wheelchair). (****) (horses)

Delton, J. *I'll Never Love Anything Ever Again*, Gr. PS-3. Chronic Illness: Allergies. (****) (dog)

Haldane, S. *Helping Hands: How Monkeys Assist People Who Are Disabled*, Gr. 3-7. Disability: Physical (wheelchair). (****) (monkey)

Hesse, K. *Lester's Dog*, Gr. PS-3. Disability: Deafness. (****) (dog & kitten)

Karim, R. *Mandy Sue Day*, Gr. PS-3. Disability: Blindness. (****) (horse)

Osofsky, A. *My Buddy*, Gr. PS-3. Disability: Physical. (****) (dog)

Porte, B. A. *Harry's Dog*, Gr. K-3. Chronic Illness: Allergies. (****) (dog)

Sanford, D. *Help! Fire!* Gr. K-3. Disability: Physical. (****) (dogs)

Simpson-Smith, E. *A Guide Dog Goes To School*, Gr. 1-3. Disability: Blindness. (****) (dog)

Spier, P. *People*, Gr. All Ages. Differences. (****)

Picnics
Raffi. *One Light, One Sun*, Gr. PS-2. Disability: Physical (wheelchair). (****)

Sargent, S., & Wirt, D.A. *My Favorite Place*, Gr. PS-3. Disability: Blindness. (****)

Planting and Gardening
Muller, G. *The Garden in the City*, Gr. 1-4. Disability: Physical. (****)

Peckinpah, S.L. *Rosey...The Imperfect Angel*, Gr. 1-3. Disability: Speech and Language (cleft lip). (***)

Safety
Brown, T. *Someone Special, Just Like You*, Gr. PS-2. Disability: Hearing, Vision, Physical, Down Syndrome. (****)

Cohen, M. *It's George*, Gr. PS-3. Disability: Slow Learner. (***)

Hearn, E. *Good Morning Franny, Good Night Franny*, Gr. PS-3. Disability: Physical (wheelchair). (****)

Macdonald, M. *Little Hippo Gets His Glasses*, Gr. PS-3. Differences. (****)

Powers, M. E. *Our Teacher's in a Wheelchair*, Gr. PS-3. Disability: Physical (wheelchair). (****)

Sanford, D. *Help! Fire!* Gr. K-3. Disability: Physical. (****)

Shapes, Sizes, Weights
Kuklin, S. *Thinking Big: The Story of a Young Dwarf*, Gr. 2-5. Disability: Physical (dwarf). (****) (size)

Morris, A. *Bread, Bread, Bread*, Gr. PS-2. Differences. (****)

Newth, P. *Roly Goes Exploring*, Gr. PS-2. Disability: Blindness (braille). (***) (shapes & sizes)

Sight (seeing)

Alexander, S. H. *Mom Can't See Me*, Gr. K-3. Disability: Blindness. (****)

Alexander, S. H. *Mom's Best Friend*, Gr. K-3. Disability: Blindness. (****)

Ancona, G., & M. B. *Handtalk Zoo*, Gr. PS-1. Disability: Deafness. (****)

Arnold, C. *A Guide Dog Puppy Grows Up*, Gr. 1-3. Disability: Blindness. (****)

Bergman, T. *We Laugh, We Live, We Cry: Children Living with Mental Retardation*, Gr. K-3. Disability: Mental Retardation. (****)

Brown, M. *Arthur's Eyes*, Gr. PS-3. Differences. (***)

Brown, T. *Someone Special, Just Like You*, Gr. PS-2. Disability: Hearing, Vision, Physical, Down Syndrome. (****)

Chaplin, S. G. *I Can Sign My ABCs*, PS-2. Disability: Deafness, Hearing Loss. (***)

Cohen, M. *See You Tomorrow*, Charles, Gr. PS-2. Disability: Blindness. (***)

Condra, E. *See The Ocean*, Gr. K-3. Disability: Blindness. (****)

Golden, B. D. *Cakes and Miracles*, Gr. K-4. Disability: Blindness. (****)

Karim, R. *Mandy Sue Day*, Gr. K-3. Disability: Blindness. (****)

Kastner, J. *Naomi knows it's springtime*, Gr. PS-2. Disability: Blindness. (****)

Macdonald, M. *Little Hippo Gets His Glasses*, Gr. PS-3. Differences. (****)

MacLachlan, P. *Through Grandpa's Eyes*, Gr. K-3. Disability: Blindness. (****)

Martin, Bill J. R. *Knots on a Counting Rope*, Gr. K-3. Disability: Blindness. (****)

Newth, P. *Roly Goes Exploring*. Gr. PS-2. Disability: Blindness (Braille). (***) (shapes & sizes)

Pearson, S. *Happy Birthday, Grampie*, Gr. PS-3. Disability: Blindness. (****)

Rankin, L. *The Handmade Alphabet*, Gr. All Ages. Disability: Deafness. (****)

Rosenberg, M. B. *My Friend Leslie: The Story of a Handicapped Child*, Gr. K-3. Disability: Multiple Disabilities: Visual, Hearing Loss, & Physical (cleft palate and muscular problems). (****)

Sargent, S. & Wirt, D. A. *My Favorite Place*, Gr. PS-3. Disability: Blindness. (***)

Simpson-Smith, E. *A Guide Dog Goes To School*, Gr. 1-3. Disability: Blindness. (****)

Slier, D. *Animal Signs: A First Book of Sign Language*, Gr. PS-K. Disability: Hearing Loss, Deafness (signing). (****)

Slier, D. *Word Signs: A First Book of Sign Language*. Gr. PS-K. Disability: Hearing Loss, Deafness (signing). (****)

Smell

Kastner, J. *Naomi knows it's springtime*, Gr. PS-2. Disability: Blindness. (****)

MacLachlan, P. *Through Grandpa's Eyes*, Gr. K-3. Disability: Blindness. (****)

Sargent, S. & Wirt, D. A. *My Favorite Place*, Gr. PS-3. Disability: Blindness. (***)

Sounds (hearing)

Bergman, T. *Going Places: Children Living with Cerebral Palsy*, Gr. PS-3. Disability: Cerebral Palsy (wheelchair) and Deafness (signing). (****)

Booth, B. *Mandy*, Gr. PS-2. Disability: Deafness. (****)

Brown, T. *Someone Special, Just Like You*, Gr. PS-2. Disability: Hearing, Vision, Physical, Down Syndrome. (****)

Chaplin, S. G. *I Can Sign My ABCs*, Gr. PS-2. Disability: Deafness. (****)

Charlip, R. *Handtalk Birthday*, Gr. K-3. Disability: Deafness. (****)

Condra, E. *See The Ocean*, Gr. K-3. Disability: Blindness. (****)

Hearn, E. *Franny and the Music Girl*, Gr. PS-2. Disability: Physical (wheelchair). (****)

Kastner, J. *Naomi knows it's springtime*, Gr. PS-2. Disability: Blindness. (****)

Lakin, P. *Dad and Me in the Morning*, Gr. PS-2. Disability: Deafness. (****)

Levi, D. *A Very Special Friend*, Gr. K-3. Disability: Deafness. (****)

Levi, D. *A Very Special Sister*, Gr. PS-2. Disability: Deafness. (****)

Levine, E. S. *Lisa And Her Soundless World*, Gr. K-3. Disability: Deafness. (****)

Litchfield, A. B. *A Button In Her Ear*, Gr. K-3. Disability: Hearing Loss. (****)

Litchfield, A.B. *Words In Our Hands*, Gr. K-3. Disability: Deafness. (****)

MacLachlan, P. *Through Grandpa's Eyes*, Gr. K-3. Disability: Blindness. (****)

Peterson, J. W. *I Have A Sister My Sister Is Deaf*, Gr. PS-3. Disability: Deafness. (***)

Rankin, L. *The Handmade Alphabet*, Gr. All Ages. Disability: Deafness (signing). (****)

Rosenberg, M. B. *My Friend Leslie: The Story of a Handicapped Child*, Gr. K-3. Disability: Multiple Disabilities: Visual, Hearing Loss, & Physical (cleft palate and muscular problems). (****)

Sargent, S. & Wirt, D. A. *My Favorite Place*, Gr. PS-3. Disability: Blindness. (***)

Slier, D. *Animal Signs: A First Book of Sign Language*. Gr. PS-K. Disability: Hearing Loss, Deafness (signing). (****)

Slier, D. *Word Signs: A First Book of Sign Language*. Gr. PS-K. Disability: Hearing Loss, Deafness (signing). (****)

Wahl, J. *Jamie's Tiger*, Gr. PS-3. Disability: Hearing Loss. (****)

Zelonski, J. *I Can't Always Hear You*, Gr. K-3. Disability: Hearing Loss. (****)

Sports
Allen, A. *Sports for the Handicapped*. Gr. 1-3. Disability: Physical, Blindness, Mental Retardation, Deafness. (***)

Kornfield, E. J. *Dreams Come True*, Gr. 1-4. Disability/Chronic Illness: Epilepsy. (figure skating). (****)

Lee, J.M. *Silent Lotus*, Gr. K-3. Disability: Deafness. (dancing). (****)

Moran, G. *Imagine Me on a Sit-Ski!* Gr. PS-3. Disability: Physical (skiing). (****)

Peckinpah, S. L. *Chester...The Imperfect All-Star*, Gr. 1-3. Disability: Physical (one leg shorter; prosthesis). (baseball). (***)

Spring
Hearn, E. *Good Morning Franny, Good Night Franny*, Gr. PS-3. Disability: Physical (wheelchair). (****)

Kastner, J. *Naomi knows it's springtime*, Gr. PS-2. Disability: Blindness. (****)

Muller, G. *A Garden in the City*, Gr. 1-4. Disability: Physical. (****)

Summer

Bunnett, R. *Friends in The Park*, Gr. PS-1. Disability: Physical, Down Syndrome. (****)

Condra, E. *See The Ocean*, Gr. K-3. Disability: Blindness. (****)

Karim, R. *Mandy Sue Day*, Gr. K-3. Disability: Blindness. (****)

Levi, D. *A Very Special Friend*, Gr. K-3. Disability: Deafness. (****)

Moss, D. M. *Lee, the Rabbit with Epilepsy*, Gr. K-4. Disability: Epilepsy. (***)

Nikola-Lisa, W. *Bein' With You This Way*, Gr. PS-3. Differences. (****)

Raffi. *One Light, One Sun*, Gr. PS-2. Disability: Physical (wheelchair). (****)

Sargent, S. & Wirt, D. A. *My Favorite Place*, Gr. PS-3. Disability: Blindness. (***)

Taste

Sargent, S. & Wirt, D. A. *My Favorite Place*, Gr. PS-3. Disability: Blindness. (***)

Tools and Machines to Use in My World

London, J. *The Lion Who Has Asthma*, Gr. PS-2. Illness: Asthma (nebulizer). (****)

Touch

Alexander, S. H. *Mom Can't See Me*, Gr. K-3. Disability: Blindness. (****)

Golden, B. D. *Cakes and Miracles*, Gr. K-4. Disability: Blindness. (****)

Holcomb, N. *Fair and Square*, Gr. PS-1. Disability: Physical (switches). (****)

Karim, R. *Mandy Sue Day*, Gr. PS-3. Disability: Blindness. (****)

Kastner, J. *Naomi Knows It's Springtime*, Gr. PS-2. Disability: Blindness. (****)

Newth, P. *Roly Goes Exploring*, Gr. PS-2. Disability: Blindness (braille). (***)

Pearson, S. *Happy Birthday, Grampie*, Gr. PS-3. Disability: Blindness. (****)

Sargent, S. & Wirt, D. A. *My Favorite Place*, Gr. PS-3. Disability: Blindness. (***)

Transportation

Baer, E. *This is the Way We Go to School*, Gr. PS-3. Differences. (****)

Damrell, L. *With The Wind*, Gr. PS-2. Disability: Physical (leg braces & wheelchair). (Horseback riding). (****)

Hearn, E. *Good Morning Franny, Good Night Franny*, Gr. PS-3. Disability: Physical (wheelchair). (****)

Holy Cross School Kindergartners. *What's Under Your Hood Orson?* Gr. PS-1. Differences. (****)

Lasker, J. *Nick Joins In*, Gr. 2-3. Disability: Physical (leg braces & wheelchair). (***)

Morris, A. *On The Go*, Gr. PS-3. Differences. (****)

Muldoon, K. M. *Princess Pooh*, Gr. 2-5. Disability: Physical (crutches, wheelchair). (****)

Powers, M. E. *Our Teacher's in a Wheelchair*, Gr. PS-3. Disability: Physical (wheelchair). (****)

Rabe, B. *The Balancing Girl*, Gr. K-3. Disability: Physical (wheelchair, leg braces, crutches). (****)

We are Alike, We are Different

Alexander, S. H. *Mom Can't See Me*, Gr. K-3. Disability: Blindness. (****)

Amenta, C. A. *Russell is Extra Special: A Book About Autism for Children*, Gr. PS-2. Disability: Autism. (****)

Arnold, C. *A Guide Dog Puppy Grows Up*, Gr. 1-3. Disability: Blindness. (****)

Badt, K.L. *Hair There and Everywhere*, Gr. 1-5. Differences. (****)

Barrett, M.B. *Sing To The Stars*, Gr. PS-3. Disability: Blindness. (****)

Bergman, T. *Going Places: Children Living with Cerebral Palsy*, Gr. PS-3. Disability: Cerebral Palsy (wheelchair) and Deafness (signing). (****)

Brown, M. *Arthur's Eyes*, Gr. PS-3. Differences. (***)

Brown, T. *Someone Special, Just Like You*, Gr. PS-2. Disability: Hearing, Vision, Physical, Down Syndrome. (****)

Bunnett, R. *Friends in The Park*, Gr. PS-1. Disability: Physical, Down Syndrome. (****)

Bunting, E. *The Wall*, Gr. PS-3. Disability: Physical. (****)

Cairo, S. *Our Brother Has Down's Syndrome*, Gr. K-3. Disability: Down Syndrome. (***)

Carlson, N. *Arnie and the New Kid*, Gr. PS-3. Disability: Physical (wheelchair). (****)

Caseley, J. *Harry and Willy and Carrothead*, Gr. K-3. Disability: Physical (prosthesis for left hand). (****)

Charlip, R. *Handtalk Birthday*, Gr. K-3. Disability: Deafness. (****)

Cheltenham Elem. School. *We Are Alike...We Are All Different*, Gr. PS-2. (****)

Cohen, M. *See You Tomorrow, Charles*, Gr. PS-2. Disability: Blindness. (***)

Condra, E. *See The Ocean*, Gr. K-3. Disability: Blindness. (****)

Damrell, L. *With The Wind*, Gr. PS-2. Disability: Physical (leg braces & wheelchair). (Horseback riding). (****)

de Poix, C. *Jo, Flo and Yolanda*, Gr. PS-3. Differences. (****)

Dorros, A. *This is My House*, Gr. PS-2. Differences. (****)

Dwight, L. *We Can Do It!* Gr. PS-2. Disability: Spina Bifida, Down Syndrome, Cerebral Palsy, Blindness. (****)

Dwyer, K. *What Do You Mean I Have A Learning Disability?* Gr. 1-5. Disability: Learning Disability. (***)

Emmert, M. *I'm The Big Sister Now*, Gr. K-3. Disability: Cerebral Palsy, Severe Brain Damage (multiple disabilities). (****)

Gehret, J. *Eagle Eyes*, Gr. 1-5. Disability/Illness: Attention Deficit Disorder. (****)

Golden, B. D. *Cakes and Miracles*, Gr. K-4. Disability: Blindness. (****)

Haines, S. *Becca and Sue Make Two*, Gr. K-3. Disability: Down syndrome. (***)

Haldane, S. *Helping Hands: How Monkeys Assist People Who Are Disabled*, Gr. 3-7. Disability: Physical (wheelchair). (****)

Hamanaka, S. *All The Colors of the World*, Gr. PS-3. Differences. (****)

Hearn, E. *Good Morning Franny, Good Night Franny*, Gr. PS-3. Disability: Physical (wheelchair). (****)

Henriod, L. *Grandma's Wheelchair*, Gr. PS-2. Disability: Physical (wheelchair). (****)

Holcomb, N. *Fair and Square*, Gr. PS-1. Disability: Physical (switches). (****)

Holcomb, N. *Patrick and Emma Lou*, Gr. PS-1. Disability: Physical (cerebral palsy, walker). (***)

Holcomb, N. *Sarah's Surprise*, PS-1. Disability: Speech/Language. (**)

Holy Cross Kindergartners. *What's Under Your Hood, Orson?* Gr. PS-1. Differences. (****)

Kornfield, E. J. *Dreams Come True*, Gr. 1-4. Disability/Chronic Illness: Epilepsy. (****)

Krisher, T. *Kathy's Hats: A Story of Hope*, Gr. PS-2. Chronic Illness: Cancer. (****)

Lasker, J. *Nick Joins In*, Gr. 2-3. Disability: Physical (leg braces and wheelchair). (***)

Leventhal, D. *What is Your Language?* Gr. PS-3. Differences. (****)

Karim, R. *Mandy Sue Day*, Gr. PS-3. Disability: Blindness. (****)

Kuklin, S. *Thinking Big: The Story of a Young Dwarf*, Gr. 2-5. Disability: Physical (dwarf). (****)

Levi, D. *A Very Special Friend*, Gr. K-3. Disability: Deafness. (****)

Levi, D. *A Very Special Sister*, Gr. PS-2. Disability: Deafness. (****)

Litchfield, A. B. *A Button In Her Ear*, Gr. K-3. Disability: Hearing Loss. (****)

Litchfield, A. B. *Making Room for Uncle Joe*, Gr. 1-4. Disability: Down Syndrome. (***)

Litchfield, A.B. *Words in Our Hands*, Gr. K-3. Disability: Deafness. (****)

Loski, D. *The Boy On The Bus*, Gr. 1-3. Disability: ADD. (****)

Macdonald, M. *Little Hippo Gets His Glasses*, Gr. PS-3. Differences. (****)

MacLachlan, P. *Through Grandpa's Eyes*, Gr. K-3. Disability: Blindness. (****)

McDonald, M. *The Potato Man*, Gr. PS-2. Differences. (****)

Martin, Bill J. R. *Knots on a Counting Rope*, Gr. K-3. Disability: Blindness. (****)

Mayer, G. & M. *A Very Special Critter*, Gr. PS-3. Disability: Physical. (****)

Merrifield, M. *Come Sit By Me*, Gr. PS-3. Chronic Illness: HIV – AIDS. (****)

Moran, G. *Imagine Me on a Sit-Ski!* Gr. PS-3. Disability: Physical, Speech and Language. (****)

Morris, A. *Bread, Bread, Bread*, Gr. PS-2. Differences. (****)

Morris, A. *Hats, Hats, Hats*, Gr. PS-2. Differences. (****)

Morris, A. *On The Go*, Gr. PS-3. Differences. (****)

Moss, D. M. *Lee, the Rabbit with Epilepsy*, Gr. K-4. Disability: Epilepsy. (***)

Moss, D. M. *Shelley The Hyperactive Turtle*, Gr. K-3. Disability: Hyperactivity. (**)

Newth, P. *Roly Goes Exploring*. Gr. PS-2. Disability: Blindness (braille). (***)

Nikola-Lisa, W. *Bein' With You This Way*, Gr. PS-3. Differences. (****)

O'Shaughnessy, E. *Somebody Called Me A Retard Today…and My Heart Felt Sad*, Gr. PS-K. Disability: Mental Retardation, Learning Disability. (****)

Osofsky, A. *My Buddy*, Gr. PS-3. Disability: Physical (muscular dystrophy). (****)

Peckinpah, S. L. *Chester…The Imperfect All-Star*, Gr. 1-3. Disability: Physical (one leg shorter; prosthesis). (***)

Peckinpah, S.L. *Rosey…The Imperfect Angel*, Gr. 1-3. Disability: Speech and Language (cleft lip). (****)

Peterson, J. W. *I Have A Sister My Sister Is Deaf*, Gr. PS-3. Disability: Deafness. (***)

Pirner, C. W. *Even Little Kids Get Diabetes*, Fiction, Gr. PS-2. Chronic Illness: Diabetes. (****)

Powers, M. E. *Our Teacher's in a Wheelchair*, Gr. PS-3. Disability: Physical (wheelchair). (****)

Quinsey, M.B. *Why Does That Man Have Such A Big Nose?* Gr. PS-3. Differences. (****)

Rabe, B. *The Balancing Girl*, Gr. PS-2. Disability: Physical (wheelchair, leg braces, crutches). (****) (red)

Rabe, B. *Where's Chimpy?* Gr. K-3. Disability: Physical (wheelchair, leg braces, crutches). (****) (monkey)

Rankin, L. *The Handmade Alphabet*, Gr. All Ages. Disability: Deafness. (****)

Rosenberg, M. B. *Finding A Way: Living with Exceptional Brothers and Sisters*, Gr. K-3. Disability/Illness: Diabetes, Asthma, & Spina Bifida. (****)

Rosenberg, M. B. *My Friend Leslie: The Story of a Handicapped Child*, Gr. K-3. Disability: Multiple Disabilities: Visual, Hearing Loss, & Physical (cleft palate and muscular problems). (****)

Russo, M. *Alex is My Friend*, Gr. PS-2. Disability: Physical (size). (****)

Sanford, D. *Don't Look at Me*, Gr. 1-3. Disability: Mental Retardation or Learning Disability. (****)

Sanford, D. *Help! Fire!* Gr. K-3. Disability: Physical. (****)

Seuling, B. *I'm Not So Different*, Gr. K-3. Disability: Physical (wheelchair). (****)

Simon, N. *All Kinds of Families*, Gr. PS-3. Differences. (****)

Simon, N. *Why Am I Different?* Gr. PS-3. Differences. (****)

Spier, P. *People*, Gr. All Ages. Differences. (****)

Swanson, S.M. *My Friend Emily*, Gr. 1-3. Disability/Illness: Epilepsy. (****)

Taylor, R. *All By Self*, Gr. K-6. Disability: Cerebral Palsy (wheelchair). (****)

Thompson, M. *My Brother Matthew*, Gr. K-3. Disability: Physical and Speech/Language Delay (brain injury). (****)

Verniero, J. *You Can Call Me Willy*, Gr. 1-4. Illness: HIV and AIDS. (****)

Wahl, J. *Jamie's Tiger*, Gr. PS-3. Disability: Hearing Loss. (****)

Whinston, J. L. *I'm Joshua & Yes I Can*, Gr. 3-6. Disability: Cerebral Palsy (leg braces). (****)

White, P. *Janet at School*, Gr. PS-2. Disability: Physical, Spina Bifida (leg braces & wheelchair). (***)

Wright, B.R. *My Sister is Different*, Gr. K-3. Disability: Mental Retardation. (****)

Wright, C. *Just Like Emma: How She Has Fun in God's World*, Gr. K-3. Disability: Physical (spina bifida). (****)

Zelonsky, J. *I Can't Always Hear You*, Gr. K-3. Disability: Hearing Loss. (****)

Wheels

Allen, A. *Sports for the Handicapped*, Gr. 1-3. Disability: Physical, Blindness, Mental Retardation, Deafness. (***)

Bennett, C. J. *Giant Steps for Steven*, Gr. K-3. Disability: Spina Bifida (leg braces, crutches, AMIGO - motorized wheelchair) (****)

Burns, K. *Our Mom*, Gr. PS-3. Disability: Physical (wheelchair). (****)

Hearn, E. *Good Morning Franny, Good Night Franny*, Gr. PS-3. Disability: Physical (wheelchair). (****)

Hearn, E. *Race You Franny*, Gr. PS-3. Disability: Physical. (****)

Henriod, L. *Grandma's Wheelchair*, Gr. PS-2. Disability: Physical (wheelchair). (****)

Lasker, J. *Nick Joins In*, Gr. 2-3. Disability: Physical (leg braces & wheelchair). (***)

Powers, M. E. *Our Teacher's in a Wheelchair*, Gr. PS-3. Disability: Physical (wheelchair). (****)

Rabe, B. *The Balancing Girl*, Gr. PS-2. Disability: Physical (wheelchair, leg braces, crutches). (****) (red)

Winter

Moran, G. *Imagine Me on a Sit-Ski!* Gr. PS-3. Disability: Physical and Speech and Language. (****)

Zoo Animals

Ancona, G. and Ancona, M. B. *Handtalk Zoo*, Gr. PS-1. Disability: Deafness. (****)

Haldane, S. *Helping Hands: How Monkeys Assist People Who Are Disabled*, Gr. 3-7. Disability: Physical (wheelchair). (****) (monkey)

London, J. *The Lion Who Has Asthma*, Gr. PS-2. Illness: Asthma. (****) (variety of jungle animals)

Rabe, B. *Where's Chimpy?* Gr. K-3. Disability: Physical (wheelchair, leg braces, crutches). (****) (monkey)

References

Harste, J. C., Short, K. G., & Burke, C. (1988). *Creating classrooms for authors.* Portsmouth, NH: Heinemann.

Heine, P. (1991). The power of related books. *The Reading Teacher*, 45(1), 75-77.

....
Notes

··············
CHAPTER TEN

Lesson Plans for Text Sets

Introduction

Sample Lesson Plans have been developed to help you organize the children's literature you choose to use with each of your themes or units. Each Lesson Plan has a space at the top to identify the Theme. Next, there are three sections for you to list children's books in the text set that relate to the theme by incorporating: 1) disabilities or chronic illness, 2) diverse cultures, and 3) other favorite books.

For the first section of the Lesson Plan, Books Incorporating Disabilities or Chronic Illness, refer to Chapter nine where the books in this collection are listed by theme or unit. Simply select books from the theme that are appropriate for the grade level(s) with whom you are working. Remember that most often children's books can be used effectively outside the recommended grade levels. Next, in section two, add your choice of books that incorporate diverse cultures and in section three, add any other favorite books related to the theme.

Once you have developed Lesson Plans for each theme that you use in your curriculum, it will be an easy task to select children's literature for your units. Merely check your Lesson Plans for the theme you will be teaching and immediately you will know which books are appropriate. Within each Text Set, you select how many books you plan to use. With this format, you will be able to continually update your Lesson Plans by adding newly published books and new favorites that you discover. Additional Lesson Plans can be developed for each new theme you choose to teach.

Sample Lesson Plans for the themes of Friends and School and Giving and Sharing are provided. An empty Lesson Plan is also provided which can be copied so you are able to develop as many Lesson Plans as you might need.

Sample Lesson Plan

Text Set Lesson Plan
Theme: Friends and School

Books incorporating disabilities or chronic illness:

Brown, Tricia. *Someone Special, Just Like You*, Gr. PS-2.
Carlson, Nancy. *Arnie and the New Kid*, Gr. PS-3.
Caseley, Judith. *Harry and Willy and Carrothead*, Gr. K-3.
Cohen, Miriam. *It's George*, Gr. PS-3.
Cohen, Miriam. *See You Tomorrow, Charles*, Gr. PS-2.
Dwight, Laura. *We Can Do It!*, Gr. PS-2.
Girard, Linda W. *Alex, the Kid with AIDS*, Gr. 1-4.
Krisher, Trudy. *Kathy's Hats: A Story of Hope*, Gr. PS-2.
Lasker, Joe. *Nick Joins In*, Gr. 2-3.
Litchfield, Ada B. *A Button In Her Ear*, Gr. K-3.
Litchfield, Ada B. *A Button In Her Ear*, Gr. K-3.
Loski, Diana. *The Boy On The Bus*, Gr. 1-3.
Mayer, Gina. & Mercer. *A Very Special Critter*, Gr. PS-3.
Merrifield, Margaret. *Come Sit By Me*, Gr. PS-3.
Rabe, Berniece. *The Balancing Girl*, Gr. K-3.
Rosenberg, Maxine. B. *My Friend Leslie: The Story of a Handicapped. Child*, Gr. K-3.
Sanford, Doris. *Don't Look At Me*, Gr. 1-3.
Verniero, J. *You Can Call Me Willy*, Gr. 1-4
Whinston, Joan Lenett. *I'm Joshua & Yes I Can*, Gr. 3-6.
Zelonski, Jill. *I Can't Always Hear You*, Gr. K-3.

_____

_____

Books incorporating diverse cultures:

_____

_____

_____

_____

_____

_____

_____

Other favorite books:

_____

_____

_____

_____

_____

_____

Sample Lesson Plan

Text Set Lesson Plan
Theme: Giving and Sharing

Books incorporating disabilities or chronic illness:
Amadeo, Diane M. *There's A Little Bit Of Me In Jamey*, Gr. 1-4.
Arnold, Caroline. *A Guide Dog Puppy Grows Up*, Gr. 1-3.
Calmenson, Stephanie. *Rosie: A Visiting Dog's Story*, Gr. PS-3.
Carlson, Nancy. *Arnie and the New Kid*, Gr. PS-3.
Charlip, Remy. *Handtalk Birthday*, Gr. K-3.
Hesse, Karen. *Lester's Dog*, Gr. PS-3.
Litchfield, Ada B. *Making Room for Uncle Joe*, Gr. 1-4.
Moon, N. *Lucy's Pictures*, Gr. PS-3
Pearson, Susan. *Happy Birthday, Grampie*, Gr. PS-3.
Rogers, Alison. *Luke Has Asthma*, Too, Gr. PS-2.
Russo, Marisabine. *Alex is My Friend*, Gr. PS-2.
Seuling, Barbara. *I'm Not So Different*, Gr. K-3.

Books incorporating diverse cultures:

Other favorite books:

Sample Lesson Plan

Text Set Lesson Plan
Theme:_____

_____

Books incorporating disabilities or chronic illness:

_____
_____
_____
_____
_____
_____
_____
_____

Books incorporating diverse cultures:

_____
_____
_____
_____
_____
_____
_____

Other favorite books:

_____
_____
_____
_____
_____
_____
_____
_____
_____
_____
_____
_____

Activities for Teaching Young Children About Disabilities

It may be difficult for young children to understand what it means to have a particular disability because they have not experienced it. Participating in simulated activities can make the abstract notion of a disability become more real and concrete, and increase the children's level of understanding. When children participate in these activities, it is important that they demonstrate respect toward persons with the disability throughout the activity (e.g. silliness and laughing should be monitored). With all of the activities, the professional should be aware of safety issues, i.e. tripping when blindfolded, and take necessary precautions to keep all activities safe. Activities are included for the disabilities of blindness, partial sight, deafness or hard of hearing, and physical impairments.

Suggested Activities – Blindness or Partial Sight

Feely Bag: Put common and uncommon objects in a bag. The children reach into the bag and identify an object without looking at it. This can emphasize the challenges of not being able to see. Even very young children are able to participate in this activity by limiting the number of objects and by using common, everyday items. Emphasize to the children the importance of their sense of touch (feeling) and the importance of our labeling items for children who are blind or partially sighted.

Listening Activity: Have children listen to recordings of environmental or animal sounds and identify what they are hearing. This can point out the importance of the sense of hearing for people who are blind the importance of our telling them what it is that they are hearing in order for them to learn.

Blindfold Activity: Have several children blindfold their eyes and move about the room. This will allow the children to have a better feel for what it would be like not to be able to see. This will point out the importance of keeping everything in the room in its place so the person who is blind will not trip or fall. Point out to the children that people who are blind learn where everything is in a room and become very independent. It's best to have several children do this at a time so no one becomes embarrassed. This activity should be done respectful or persons who are blind and not with silliness or as a joke.

Tasting Party: Have a variety of bite sized foods for children to taste. With the children blindfolded, see if they can identify what they are eating from taste and smell only. To make it more difficult have foods that are very similar like a cookie and a cracker or two different kinds of juice. This will point out the importance of using these two additional senses.

Food Discovery: For children who can tell time, explain the system used by people who are blind to find food on their dinner plate. They pretend the plate is a clock and the food is placed at 12:00, 3:00, 6:00 and 9:00. On each student's plate, place four different kinds of bite sized food at these four respective times. Each plate should have the food in the same order so you can work with several children at once. Together the children try to identify the food at 3:00, the food at 9:00 etc. Or you could instruct the children to find and identify the food at 12;00, at 6:00, etc.

Aids and Equipment: Collect as many aids used by blind and partially sighted people as possible. Provide times when the children can investigate and use each of the aids. Examples of possible aids are the Braille alphabet, Braille prereading activities, Braille books or books with print and Braille, bell ball, tactile ball (ball with each section a different texture), slate and stylus, Braille typewriter and white cane. A good resource is your special teacher or vision specialist.

Braille: Young children can learn one or two letters in Braille. A good letter to begin with is the first letter in their names. Older children may be able to learn all of the letters in their names. Children enjoy seeing what their own name looks like in Braille even if learning the entire name is too difficult. This allows the children to appreciate how challenging it can be to learn to read Braille with your fingers. Again, your best resource in the vision consultant.

Suggested Activities – Deafness or Hearing Impairment

Story Time With a Hearing Loss: Have the children listen to a taped story or a video with the sound turned down so low it becomes very difficult to understand what is being said. This will simulate a hearing loss. Then listen to the tape or video again with the sound turned up. Talk to the children about what it was like and how they felt when they couldn't quite hear the story.

Story time with Deafness: Use the taped story or a video with no sound. Then read to the children by mouthing the words. Children will begin to understand what it means to be deaf and why it is important to see a person's face when he or she is speaking in order to read the lips.

Aids and Equipment: Provide the children with the opportunity to investigate and experience equipment that is used by persons with a hearing loss (e.g. hearing aids, phonic ear). Your best resource is the teacher of the hearing impaired or a speech and language clinician.

Snack Time with Gestures: During snack time, have several choices of snacks for the children and make the rule that they must communicate with gestures only. They will need to tell you which snack items they want and how many by gesturing. This will help the children realize how difficult it is to communicate without speaking and appreciate the need for alternate means of communication, i.e. sign, lip reading and communication boards.

Snack Time with Sign Language: Teach the children some easy signs that can be used during snack time such as the signs for drink, more, thank you and toilet. Require the children to communicate during this period of time with only sign language. Children enjoy learning some signs and come to realize that there are different ways to communicate.

Suggested Activities – Physical Impairments

Aids and Equipment: Provide opportunities for children to experience the aids that are used by persons with physical impairments. Examples of equipment that may be borrowed or rented are: crutches, leg braces, a wheelchair, walking sticks, a stander, adaptive eating utensils, etc. Good resources for you are special education, your occupational therapist or physical therapist. Some stores that rent equipment will allow schools to borrow items for short periods of time.

Wheelchair Maze: If a wheelchair is available, set up a short path for the children to follow including some obstacles. This will help them understand how independent a person in a wheelchair can be until an obstacle in the environment gets in the way. With the children, problem-solve how to overcome the obstacle. By wheeling around the classroom, the children become aware of the importance of keeping the room in a particular arrangement to make room for the chair and having items at a height that can be reached by a person in a wheelchair.

Paint With Your Feet: Some times when people have a physical disability that takes away the use of their arms and hands, they learn to use their feet for drawing, painting and even eating. Children could try painting with their feet by holding the brush with their toes and using watercolor paints and large paper as they experiment. This exercise would allow them to see how difficult it is, yet it can be learned with perseverance.

Suggested Activities – Mental Retardation or Learning Disability

(Simulation for these disabilities is much more difficult.)

Symbols for Letters: For children who can read, substitute symbols for the letters of the alphabet. Give the children a short sentence to read. In order for them to read each word, they must first look up each symbol and find out which letter it stands for. This is difficult and time consuming which is what happens to students who have challenges with learning.

Reading At A Higher Level: Again this activity is for children who can read. Give them some sentences or a short paragraph to read from a higher reading level than they are performing. Because they won't know many of the words, this task will be difficult and frustrating which again is what happens to students who have challenges learning.

Suggested Activities – For All Ages

Use Dolls or Stuffed Animals: To integrate information about disabilities throughout the curriculum, it is important to have dolls or stuffed animals that represent a variety of disabilities routinely available for children during play time. Much as we should have dolls that represent a variety of cultures, we should have dolls that represent a variety of disabilities. More and more school supply catalogs have dolls available for purchase.

Story Telling With Persona Dolls: Each persona doll will have his or her own life story. The stories provide a way for introducing differences that do not exist in your classroom that would include persons with disabilities. In this way, children get to meet a doll with a disability, have an opportunity to ask questions and become comfortable with this disability. You can make up your own stories about issues relevant to your class. Additional stories are available from Kay Taus at Seeds university elementary School, UCLA, 405 Hilgard Ave., Los Angeles, CA 90024.

Resources

Chapel Hill Training Outreach Project, 800 East Town D, Suite 105, Chapel Hill, NC 27514.
This project provides easy to follow patterns for making dolls including those with disabilities.

Froschle, M., Colon, L., Rubin, E., & Sprung, B. (1984). *Including all of us: An early childhood curriculum about disability.* New York: Educational Equity Concepts, Inc.
This is an excellent curriculum that teaches about differences and disability. Information is provided for the teacher and activities appropriate for young children are included for each disability area.

Hal's Pals, P.O. Box 3490, Winter Park, CO 80482. (303)726-8388.
Soft sculpture dolls are available depicting children with disabilities. They will accept custom orders.

PACER Center, Inc. (Parent Advocacy Coalition for Educational Rights), 4826 Chicago Ave. So., Minneapolis, MN 55417-1055, (800)-53PACER.
This organization has a set of large puppets representing children with disabilities. The puppets are of exceptional quality and are used by their volunteers who go into schools and teach children about various disabilities. The PACER puppets are available for purchase.

Pediatric Projects Inc., PO Box 571555, Tarzana, CA 91357-1555, (800) 947-0947. FAX (818)705-3660.
This is a nonprofit public benefit corporation that distributes medical toys for children. They have developed a 20" soft-sculpture doll with Down syndrome. The doll has durable fabric, moveable arms and legs, hair, clothing and can be washed. Approximate cost $75.00.

People of Every Stripe! P.O. Box 12505, Portland, OR 97212. (503)282-0612.
This catalog has many dolls that represent a variety of cultures and disabilities.

Notes

Publishers of Children's Books

Abingdon Press
201 Eighth Avenue South
Nashville, TN 37202
(800) 251-3320

Albert Whitman & Co.
6340 Oakton St.
Morton Grove, IL 60053-2723
(800) 255-7675

Alfred A. Knopf, Inc.
225 Park Avenue So.
New York, NY 10003
(800) 733-3000

Alyson Publications, Inc.
40 Plymouth St.
Boston, MA 02118
(617) 542-5679

Annick Press LTD.
Distributed by Firefly Books Ltd.
P.O. Box 1338
Elicott Station
Buffalo, NY 14205
(800) 387-5085

Augsburg Fortress Publishers
426 South Fifth Street
Box 1209
Minneapolis, MN 55440
(612) 330-3300
(800) 328-4648

Boyds Mills Press, Inc.
815 Church Street
Honesdale, PA 18431
(717) 253-1164

Checkerboard Press
30 Vesey St.
New York, NY 10007
(212) 571-6300

Children's Press
5440 N. Cumberland Avenue
Chicago, IL 60656
(800) 621-1115

Clarion Press
215 Park Avenue So.
New York, NY 10003
(800) 733-1717

Crown Publishers, Inc.
201 East 50th St.
New York, NY 10022
(800) 726-0600

Dasan Productions Inc.
PO Box 300
Agara Hills, CA 91376
(800) 348-4401

Dell Publishing
1540 Broadway
New York, NY 10036
(800) 223-6834

Dial Books for Young Readers
375 Hudson Street
New York, NY 10014
(212) 366-2000

Dillon Press
Division of MacMillian Publishing Co.
Inc.
866 Third Avenue No.
New York, NY 10022
(800) 257-5755

Dinasaur Publications
Division of Harper Collins Publishers Ltd.
10 E. 53rd St.
New York, NY 10022-5299
(800) 328-3443

Dutton Children's Books
375 Hudson Street
New York, NY 10014
(212) 366-2000

Farrar, Straus & Giroux
19 Union Square West
New York, NY 10003
(800) 631-8571

Franklin Watts
95 Madison Avenue
New York, NY 10016
(800) 672-6672

Gareth Stevens, Inc.
1555 N. River Center Dr.
Milwaukee, Wisconsin 53212
(800) 341-3569

Greenwillow Books
1350 Avenue of the Americas
New York, NY 10019
(800) 843-9389

Harcourt Brace & Company
1250 6th Avenue
San Diego, CA 92101
(800) 346-8648

Harper Collins Publishers
10 East 53rd Street
New York, NY 10022-5299
(800) 328-3443

Harper Trophy
10 East 53rd Street
New York, NY 10022
(800) 328-3443

Henry Holt & Co.
115 West 18th Street
New York, NY 10011
(800) 448-5233

Human Sciences Press
233 Spring Street
New York, NY 10013
(800) 221-9369

Ideal's Childrens Books
PO Box 140300
Nashville, TN 37214
(800) 327-5113

Jason & Nordic Publishers
PO Box 441
Holidaysburg, PA 16648
(814) 696-2920

Kane/Miller Book Publishers
PO Box 529
Brooklyn, NY 11231
(718) 624-5120

Kendal Green Publisher
Gallaudet University Press
800 Florida Ave., N.E.
Washington, DC 20002-3695
(202) 651-5488
(800) 451-1073 TDD

Lee & Low Books, Ind.
228 East 45th Street
New York, NY 10017
(800) 788-3123

Light On Books & Videotapes
PO Box 8005, Suite 358
Boulder, CO 80306
(303) 444-7125

Little, Brown & Company
1271 Avenue of the Americas
New York, NY 10020
(800) 759-0190

Lothrop, Lee & Shepard Bks.
1350 Avenue of the Americas
New York, NY 10019
(800) 237-0657

Macmillan Publishing Co.
866 3rd Avenue
New York, NY 10022
(800) 257-5755

Magination Press
19 Union Square West
New York, NY 10003
(212) 924-3344

Melius Publishers, Inc.
118 River road
Pierre, SD 57501
(800) 882-5171

William Morrow & Co., Inc.
1350 Avenue of the Americas
New York, NY 10019
(800) 237-0657

Multnomah Press Books
PO Box 3720
Sisters, OR 97759
(503) 549-1144

Orchard Books
95 Madison Ave., 11th Floor
New York, NY 10016
(800) 672-6672

Parenting Press, Inc.
PO Box 75267
Seattle, WA 98125
(800) 992-6657

Philomel Books
Division of Putnam & Grosset Group
200 Madison Avenue
New York, NY 10016
(800) 631-8571

G. P. Putnam's Sons
200 Madison Avenue
New York, NY 10016
(800) 631-8571

Raintree Steck-Vaughn
11 Prospect St.
Madison, NJ 07940
(800) 558-7264

Random Books for Young Readers
201 E. 50th Street
New York, NY 10022
(800) 733-3000

Rocky Mountain Children's Press
1520 Shaw Mountain Road
Boise, ID 83712
(208) 336-3858

Scholastic, Inc.
PO Box 7502
Jefferson City, MO 65102
(800) 631-1586

Second Story Press
Division of Inland Book Co.
PO Box 120470
East Haven, CT 06512
(800) 253-3605

Vantage Press
516 West 34th Street
New York, NY 10001
(800) 882-3273

Verbal Images Press
19 Fox Hill Drive
Fairport, New York 14450
(716) 377-5401

Viking Penguin
375 Hudson Street
New York, NY 10014-3657
(800) 331-4624

Walker & Co.
720 Fifth Avenue
New York, NY 10019
(800) 289-2553

Waterfront Books
85 Cresent Road
Burlington, VT 05401
(800) 639-6063

Western Publishing Co., Inc.
5945 Erie St.
Racine, Wisconsin 53402
(800) 225-9514

Woodbine House
5615 Fishers Lane
Rockville, MD 20852
(800) 843-7323

Writer's Press Service
5278 Chinden Blvd.
Boise, Idaho 83714
(208) 327-0566

···········

APPENDIX C

Children's Books That Include Persons with Disabilities or Illnesses Alphabetized by Title

Alef-bet – A Hebrew Alphabet Book, Michelle Edwards
Alex Is My Friend, Marisabina, Russo
Alex, The Kid With AIDS, Linda Walvoord Girard
All By Self, Ron Taylor
Animal Signs: A First Book of Sign Language, Debby Slier
Anna's Silent World, Bernard Wolf
Apple Pie And Onions, Judith Caseley
Arnie And The New Kid, Nancy Carlson
Balancing Girl, Berniece Rabe
Be A Friend, Lori Wiener, Aprille Best, & Philip Pizzo
Becca and Sue Make Two, Sandra Haines
Boy On The Bus, Diana Loski
Boy's Best Friend, Joan Alden
Button in Her Ear, Ada B. Litchfield
Cakes and Miracles, Barbara Diamond Golden
Cecil's Story, George Ella Lyon
Chester…The Imperfect All-Star, Sandra Lee Peckinpah
Come Sit By Me, Margaret Merrifield
Dad and Me in the Morning, Patricia Lakin
Daddy & Me, Jeanne Montoussamy-Ashe
David Has AIDS, Doris Sanford
Don't Look at Me, Doris Sanford
Dreams Come True, Elizabeth J. Kornfield
Eagle Eyes, Jeanne Gehret
Even Little Kids Get Diabetes, Donnie White Pirner
Fair And Square, Nan Holcomb
Finding A Way: Living with Exceptional Brothers & Sisters, M. B. Rosenberg
Franny And The Music Girl, Emily Hearn
Friends In The Park, Rochelle Bunnett
Garden in the City, Gerda Muller
Going Places: Children Living with Cerebral Palsy, Thomas Bergman
Good Morning Franny, Good Night Franny, Emily Hearn
Gramma's Walk, Anna Grossnickle Hines
Grandma Drives A Motor Bed, Diane Johnson Hamm
Grandma's Wheelchair, Lorraine Henriod
Guide Dog Goes To School, S. Sargent, D.A. Wirt, & E. Simpson-Smith
Guide Dog Puppy Grows Up, Caroline Arnold
Handmade Alphabet, Laura Rankin
Handtalk Birthday, Remy Charlip
Handtalk Zoo, George & Mary Beth Ancona

Happy Birthday, Grampie, Susan Pearson
Harry And Willy And Carrothead, Judith Caseley
Harry's Dog, Barbara Ann Porte
Help! Fire! Doris Sanford
Helping Hands: How Monkeys Assist People Who Are Disabled, S. Haldane
He's My Brother, Joe Lasker
I Can Sign My ABCs, Susan Gibbons Chaplin
I Can't Always Hear You, Joy Zelonsky
I Have A Sister My Sister Is Deaf, Jeanne Whitehouse Peterson
I Have Diabetes, Althea
I'll Never Love Anything Ever Again, Judy Delton
I'm Joshua & Yes I Can, Joan Lenett Whinston
I'm Not So Different, Barbara Seuling
I'm The Big Sister Now, Michelle Emmert
Imagine Me On A Sit-Ski! George Moran
It's George, Miriam Cohen
Jamie's Tiger, Jan Wahl
Janet At School, Paul White
Just Like Emma: How She Has Fun in God's World, Christine Wright
Kathy's Hats: A Story of Hope, Trudy Krisher
Knots on a Counting Rope, Bill J.R. Martin
Lee, the Rabbit with Epilepsy, Deborah M. Moss
Lester's Dog, Karen Hesse
Lion Who Has Asthma, Jonathan London
Lisa and Her Soundless World, Edna S. Levine
Losing Uncle Tim, MaryKate Jordon
Lucy's Picture, Nicola Moon
Luke Has Asthma, Alison Rogers
Making Room for Uncle Joe, Ada B. Litchfield
Mama Zooms, Jane Cowen-Fletcher
Mandy, Barbara Booth
Mandy Sue Day, Roberta Karim
Mom's Best Friend, Sally Hobart Alexander
Mom Can't See Me, Sally Hobart Alexander
My Book For Kids With Cansur, Jason Gaes
My Brother Matthew, Mary Thompson
My Buddy, Audrey Osofsky
My Friend Emily, Susanne M. Swanson
My Friend Leslie: The Story of a Handicapped Child, Maxine B. Rosenberg
My Sister is Different, Betty Ren Wright
Naomi Knows It's Springtime, Jill Kastner
Nick Joins In, Joe Lasker
One Light, One Sun, Raffi
Our Brother Has Down's Syndrome, Shelley Cairo
Our Teacher's In A Wheelchair, Mary Ellen Powers
Patrick And Emma Lou, Nan Holcomb
Princess Pooh, Kathleen M. Muldoon
Roly Goes Exploring, Philip Newth
Rosey: A Visiting Dog's Story, Stephanie Calmenson

Rosey...The Imperfect Angel, Sandra Lee Peckinpah
Runaway Sugar: All About Diabetes, A. Ivin Silverstein
Russell is Extra Special: A book About Autism for Children, C.A. Amenta
Sadako, Eleanor Coerr
Sarah's Surprise, Nan Holcomb
See The Ocean, Estelle Condra
See You Tomorrow, Charles, Miriam Cohen
Shelley The Hyperactive Turtle, Deborah M. Moss
Silent Lotus, Jeanne M. Lee
Sing To The Stars, Mary Brigid Barrett
Someone Called Me A Retard Today...and My Heart Felt Sad, E. O'Shaughnessy
Someone Special, Just Like You, Tricia Brown
Sports for the Handicapped, Anne Allen
Sunshine Home, Eve Bunting
There's A Little Bit Of Me in Jamey, Diane M. Amadeo
Thinking Big: The Story Of A Young Dwarf, Susan Kuklin
Through Grandpa's Eyes, Patricia MacLachlan
Tiger Flowers, Patricia Quinlan
Very Special Critter, Gina & Mercer Mayer
Very Special Friend, Dorothy Hoffman Levi
Very Special Sister, Dorothy Hoffman Levi
Wall, Eve Bunting
We Can Do It! Laura Dwight
We Laugh, We Love, We Cry: Children Living with Mental Retardation, Bergman
What Do You Mean I Have A Learning Disability? Kathleen Dwyer
Where's Chimpy? Berniece Rabe
William And The Good Old Days, Eloise Greenfield
With the Wind, Liz Damrell
Word Signs: A First Book of Sign Language, Debby Slier
Words In Our Hands, Ada Litchfield
You Can Call Me Willy, Joan Verniero

Notes

APPENDIX D
Key Organizations and Resources

A number of key organizations are listed for the disability areas and chronic illnesses that are represented in this collection of children's literature. If additional information is needed on any of the disabilities or illnesses contact the national organizations. Ask if there is a state or local chapter near you. The national organizations will guide you toward finding additional information and resources.

AIDS National Interfaith Network (ANIN)
110 Maryland Avenue, N.E., Suite 504
Washington, DC 20002
(202) 546-0807

AIDS Resource Foundation for Children
182 Roseville Avenue
Newark, NJ 07107
(201) 483-4250

American Association on Mental Retardation
1719 Kalorama Road N.W.
Washington, DC
(202) 387-1968

American Cancer Society
219 East 42nd St.
New York, NY 10017
(212) 726-3030

American Council for the Blind
1010 Vermont Ave. N.W., Suite 1100
Washington, DC 20005
(202) 393-3666.
(800) 424-8666

American Diabetes Association
18 East 48th Street
New York, NY 10017
(800) 232-3472

American Foundation for the Blind
15 West 16th Street
New York, NY 10011
(212) 620-2000
(800) 232-5463

American Graham Bell Association for the Deaf (AGBA)
3417 Volta Place N.W.
Washington, DC 20007
(202) 337-5220 Voice/TDD

American Speech-Language-Hearing Association
10801 Rockville Pike
Rockville, MD 20852
(301) 897-5700

Association for Children and Adults with Learning Disabilities
4156 Library Road
Pittsburgh, PA 15234
(412) 341-1515

Association for the Care of Children's Health (ACCH)
7910 Woodmont Ave., Suite 300
Bethesda, MD 20814
(301) 654-6549

Autism National Committee
7 Teresa Circle, Arlington, MA 02174
(407) 795-1894
(617) 648-1813

Autism Society of America
8601 Georgia Ave., Suite 503
Silver Spring, MD 20910
(301) 565-0433

Better Hearing Institute
Hearing Helpline
P.O. Box 1840
Washington, DC 20013
(800) 424-8576

Cancer Information Service
(800) 4-CANCER (National Line)

Candlelighters,
Childhood Cancer Foundation
2nd Floor, 1312 - 18th St. N.W.
Washington, DC 20036
(800) 366-2223

Children and Adults with Attention Deficit Disorder (C.H.A.D.D.)
499 70th Avenue N.W., Suite 308
Plantation, FL 33317
(305) 287-3700)

Cleft Palate Foundation
1218 Grandview Avenue
Pittsburgh, PA 15211
(800) 242-5338

Epilepsy Foundation of America
4351 Garden City Drive, Suite 406
Landover, MD 20785
(301) 459-3700
(800) EFA-1000

Federation for Children with Special Needs
95 Berkeley St., Suite 104
Boston, MA 02116
(617) 482-2915

Foundation for Children with Learning Disability
99 Park Ave., 6th Floor
New York, NY 10016
(212) 492-8755
(212) 687-7211

Human Growth Foundation
4720 Montgomery Lane
Bethesda, MD 20814
(301) 656-7540

Juvenile Diabetes Foundation International
432 Park Avenue South
New York, NY 10016
(800) 533-2873

Learning Disabilities Association of America (LDA)
4156 Library Road
Pittsburgh, PA 15234
(412) 341-1515
(412) 341-8077

Leukemia Society of America
211 East 43rd St.
New York, NY 10017
(212) 573-8484

Lung Line Information Services (for asthma or allergies)
National Jewish Center for Immunology and Respiratory Medicine
1400 Jackson Street
Denver, CO 80206
(800) 222-5864

March of Dimes Birth Defects Foundation
1275 Mamaroneck Avenue
White Plains, NY 10605
(914) 428-7100

Muscular Dystrophy Association (MDA)
3561 E. Sunrise
Tucson, AZ 85718
(212) 586-0808

National AIDS Hotline
(800) 342-AIDS
Spanish Access (800) 4342-AIDS
Deaf Access, TTY/TDD: (800) 243-7889

National AIDS Information Clearinghouse
P.O. Box 6003
Rockville, MD 20850
(800) 458-5231
TTY/TDD (800) 243-7012

National Association for Asthma
PO Box 30069
Tucson, AZ 855751
(602) 323-6046

National Association for the Deaf
814 Thayer Ave.
Silver Spring, MD 20910
(301) 587-1788

National Arc (formerly National Association for Retarded Citizens)
500 E. Border St., Suite 300
Arlington, TX 76011
(817) 640-0204
(800) 433-5255

National Association of People with AIDS
1413 - K Street N.W.
Washington, DC 20005
(202) 898-0414